W9-ADH-241

Learning at Not-School

This report was made possible by grants from the John D. and Catherine
T. MacArthur Foundation in connection with its grant making initiative
on Digital Media and Learning. For more information on the initiative
visit http://www.macfound.org.

The John D. and Catherine T. MacArthur Foundation Reports on Digital Media and Learning

Peer Participation and Software: What Mozilla Has to Teach Government, by David R. Booth

The Future of Learning Institutions in a Digital Age, by Cathy N. Davidson and David Theo Goldberg with the assistance of Zoë Marie Jones

The Future of Thinking: Learning Institutions in a Digital Age, by Cathy N. Davidson and David Theo Goldberg with the assistance of Zoë Marie Jones

Kids and Credibility: An Empirical Examination of Youth, Digital Media Use, and Information Credibility, by Andrew J. Flanagin and Miriam Metzger with Ethan Hartsell, Alex Markov, Ryan Medders, Rebekah Pure, and Elisia Choi

New Digital Media and Learning as an Emerging Area and "Worked Examples" as One Way Forward, by James Paul Gee

Digital Media and Technology in Afterschool Programs, Libraries, and Museums, by Becky Herr-Stephenson, Diana Rhoten, Dan Perkel, and Christo Sims with contributions from Anne Balsamo, Maura Klosterman, and Susana Smith Bautista

Living and Learning with New Media: Summary of Findings from the Digital Youth Project, by Mizuko Ito, Heather Horst, Matteo Bittanti, danah boyd, Becky Herr-Stephenson, Patricia G. Lange, C. J. Pascoe, and Laura Robinson with Sonja Baumer, Rachel Cody, Dilan Mahendran, Katynka Z. Martínez, Dan Perkel, Christo Sims, and Lisa Tripp

Young People, Ethics, and the New Digital Media: A Synthesis from the Good-Play Project, by Carrie James with Katie Davis, Andrea Flores, John M. Francis, Lindsay Pettingill, Margaret Rundle, and Howard Gardner

Confronting the Challenges of Participatory Culture: Media Education for the 21st Century, by Henry Jenkins (P.I.) with Ravi Purushotma, Margaret Weigel, Katie Clinton, and Alice J. Robison

The Civic Potential of Video Games, by Joseph Kahne, Ellen Middaugh, and Chris Evans

Quest to Learn: Developing the School for Digital Kids, by Katie Salen, Robert Torres, Loretta Wolozin, Rebecca Rufo-Tepper, and Arana Shapiro

Learning at Not-School: A Review of Study, Theory, and Advocacy for Education in Non-Formal Settings, by Julian Sefton-Green

Learning at Not-School

A Review of Study, Theory, and Advocacy for Education in Non-Formal Settings

Julian Sefton-Green

The MIT Press
Cambridge, Massachusetts
London, England

MIT Press books may be purchased at special quantity discounts for business or sales promotional use. For information, please email special_sales@mitpress.mit.edu or write to Special Sales Department, The MIT Press, 55 Hayward Street, Cambridge, MA 02142.

This book was set in Stone Sans and Stone Serif by the MIT Press. Printed and bound in the United States of America.

Library of Congress Cataloging-in-Publication Data

Sefton-Green, Julian.
Learning at not-school: a review of study, theory, and advocacy for education in non-formal settings / Julian Sefton-Green.
    p.   cm.—(The John D. and Catherine T. MacArthur Foundation reports on digital media and learning)
Includes bibliographical references.
ISBN 978-0-262-51824-6 (pbk. : alk. paper)
1. After-school programs—Cross-cultural studies. 2. Learning—Cross-cultural studies. 3. Comparative education. I. Title.
LC34.S44   2012
371.19—dc23
                                                                2012016213

10 9 8 7 6 5 4 3 2 1

Contents

Series Foreword

The John D. and Catherine T. MacArthur Foundation Reports on Digital Media and Learning, published by the MIT Press in collaboration with the Monterey Institute for Technology and Education (MITE), present findings from current research on how young people learn, play, socialize, and participate in civic life. The Reports result from research projects funded by the MacArthur Foundation as part of its $50 million initiative in digital media and learning. They are published openly online (as well as in print) in order to support broad dissemination and to stimulate further research in the field.

1 Introduction

This report investigates the study of a paradox—not a paradox in a grand theoretical tradition but more a contradiction in how we both think about and organize learning in places that are like schools but not schools.

In general terms, compulsory mass schooling—which is pretty standard across most of the world—is how most societies invest in the education of young people as their future citizens and workers. Schools are the places where young people go to get an education. Yet, despite the consensus that virtually all of us support schools in that we attend them, pay for them, and send our children there, it is universally acknowledged across the social spectrum that schools in and of themselves are not the end-all and be-all of education.

This is only the first part of the paradox: that even being successful at school is clearly not the same thing as having a satisfactory education. Young people from affluent families are likely to take part in a range of after-school activities, some private, such as music lessons and ballet classes, some community-based, such as Boy Scouts and Girl Scouts. Many employers are often vociferously skeptical about what young people learn at schools, maintaining that the young and newly employed have to learn on the job and be trained to acquire the skills needed in the workplace. Religious families often study and receive instruction in various kinds of supplementary education. Parents of young children often regard their direction of activities in the home as the child's primary education, and self-taught people often refer to the "university of life" signaling that formal qualifications have had little or no bearing on their life course.

These are but a few of the many ways in which everyday talk about the value of education is often skeptical and critical. This isn't to say that schools are worthless and unsuccessful, although many people talk about their own schooling experiences and of their children's as though the schools were of little worth; much public commentary and representation on film and TV frequently show schools as alienating, pointless environments and the last place in the world where you might learn anything. This also just isn't true.

The debates about school aren't always coherent or sensible, and there are many levels to the discussion: we will return to parts of the debate in the following chapters. Here I want to draw out two key propositions. The first is how we tend to conflate the idea of education and schools, and the second is how we often don't disentangle learning and formal education. Both of these kinds of lapses in thinking are part of how we might talk about young people in society at a general level: they are, however, inaccurate in ways that matter.

While the outcomes of education through schooling are important in the forms of credentials, or of achieving graduation status, there is also a common sense that argues that these are only proxy measures of learning, that what people *really know and can do* can't really be measured by these catch-all and fallible forms of measurement. At the same time, we all know from everyday experience that we can learn much more than simply the formal knowledge and subjects that are taught in school. Some of what we might learn might be quite complex and technical—such as fixing cars, cooking, and sorting out home Wi-Fi networks—and of course we learn throughout our lives whether it be from the more immeasurable experience of "life," such as figuring out how to raise children, and how to get along with difficult people, as well as taking on management responsibilities and whole new skillsets in forms of work that we never learned at school.

It is also true that despite the public debate suggesting that schools, education, and learning are inadequate, there are very few people who could successfully argue the opposite case: that schools do equal education, that formal education is all you need to know, and that formal education is the sole pathway to learning. Whatever people might think in private or however they provide for their own children, the language of public and political debate is, to my mind and many other scholars of education, disturbingly limited. To some extent the frame for political debate does revolve around money—who should pay how much for what kinds of programs and how to assess their value both in terms of cost and benefit to individuals, community, and the wider economy. As it is accepted that schools are a "public good" and that society benefits from the education of all, education institutions consume a world average of around 4 percent of GDP,[1] which makes clear that it is difficult for politicians to either de- or over-value this kind of expenditure.

Schools aren't just about education in the narrow sense of acquiring knowledge or learning skills; they are also key places where the young learn social behavior and where attitudes, expectations, values, and norms are transmitted, acquired, negotiated, or rejected. As Ian Hunter has shown, they were places developed in conjunction with changes in the labor force and are places of control and surveillance as well as protection and safety (Hunter 1994).

These latter socializing or moral functions stem directly from how schools are organized and the way in which their order— regular classes with horizontally arranged age grouping all learning at a similar rate, pace, and direction—exemplify a particular kind of discipline, a discipline that has inevitably affected how all of us think, feel, and identify with various social values.

And, finally, in this analysis of our understanding of what schools do, we need to take into account their importance in promising betterment. In the last half of the twentieth century, success in education was seen as the key route to higher salaries and thus offered routes to escaping poverty or, depending on your starting point, improving earning power. Many studies point to how more educated people appear to benefit from better health and social outcomes in addition to financial wealth.[2]

We need to lay out what I think of as the commonsensical and widely understood notion of how schools work. The focus in this report is those organizations or institutions (some of which are as old as schooling itself) that have grown up parallel to public schools and embed some of this common sense. I will describe how some of these institutions have developed as complements, supplements, or even attempts to remediate the alleged failures of schools. These organizations, however, set out in many cases to be different from schools and embody different purposes as well as aspiring to offer different ways of valuing learning. How we apply our norms of school, education, and learning to these institutions is crucial to how we understand how they work.

The Field of "Not-School"

In essence this report is concerned with funded, organized provision for young people that take place during out-of-school hours, and specifically with understanding the learning that goes on in such centers. First, however, we must tease out their institutional structure, their relation to funding, and how these kinds of institutions fit into an overall *ecology* of learning opportunities for young people.

Defining these kinds of institutions is tricky, given the variety of these centers, and complicated even more by cross-national comparisons, in that different countries have different ways of organizing out-of-school learning. Comparing these traditions is not straightforward and therefore greatly affects what we might mean by out-of-school centers.

After-School and Youth Community Subsectors
In the United States (and the United Kingdom) there is a conventional demarcation between after-school programs and youth community projects. After-school enrichment programs

are usually offered to children ages 10 and younger, and often take place within school buildings. They can be staffed by daytime teachers or may involve appropriately qualified para-professionals. Curricula can either be school- or play-based. Children often attend these centers as part of their childcare arrangements. Youth programs usually take place in other kinds of settings. Attendance is voluntary and usually offered to young adults. In the United Kingdom, for example, the ages range from 14 to 25. Curricula are often interest-led and frequently involve arts, media, or sporting activities as the organizing principle. Adult workers might have youth-work qualifications but are more likely to be from the communities of interest (such as artists and basketball players) or of place (such as a YMCA).

The difference between these subsectors is partly a result of targeting different age and social groups but also of differing aims and social functions. Both types of programs are likely to have different kinds of staff and different criteria for organizing activity as well as for definitions of success or quality. However, both types of programs are likely to be funded mainly from private funds, philanthropic charities or trusts, or even universities, and are less likely to have support from federal or state funds or even local-based taxation. They are both likely to receive discretionary funding from government sources, but these grants are often awarded as a result of a competitive application processes. In the United Kingdom, some after-school programs have been funded through specific grants in addition to core funding to develop expanded and extended learning opportunities in schools.

Funding

By contrast, many other European countries are likely to fund programs at national, state (regional), or at the local level, and even from supranational funds available through the European Union. This kind of funding has a long history. Some types of after-school programs are mandated through statutory provision. In Norway, for example, many local authorities provide out-of-school centers for young people who have completed their statutory qualifications that offer some catch-up learning, along with opportunities to develop interests and skills that are not generally part of the school curriculum. The level of quality and commitment of these centers is unheard of in the United States and the United Kingdom. From an international perspective, that this divergence and diversity of funding and organization exists within the local ecologies of educational programs is startling, and there are very few, if any, comparative international studies and thus very little understanding of what might comprise the key elements in any structural analysis. In addition, by definition, funders (private, philanthropic, and public) often have aims, ambitions, and obligations both to their stakeholders and to the young people they may be supporting. Both advocates and critics of funding out-of-school initiatives scrutinize accounts of impact. Funders therefore tend to develop forms of measurement and analysis that frame the learning in ways that can be measured—even where learning isn't necessarily a primary objective of the initiative. These inevitably are derived from some of the understandings about learning as defined by the common sense of schooling, described above. One major source of tension is about initiatives that are led and developed as bottom-up projects—those that have been initiated through grassroots efforts but have then sought funding from funders who may have different agendas from the project's founders and who seek to impose these more formal metrics of achievement.

The fact that organizations are "not-school" however much they operate as an image of mainstream schools in terms of system, structure, and discipline doesn't of course give them coherence as a sector or homogeneity in institutional form or scope. While it is customary for us to generalize about what "school" is, so that shared understanding of process, structure, forms of organization, personnel, and activity might be understood across most of the globe, the same generalizations cannot be made about institutions that are *not* school.

What Is Learning in Not-School?

Although casual visitors to many out-of-school centers may see forms of learning going on that resemble what they are used to, we need to be careful about assuming that such activity is a result of the organizational structure. First, as we already know, young people will behave according to the norms of conventional schooling and reiterate the kind of common sense about what defines learning, as we have already described. Their experience and understanding of not-school derives from what it is not as much as what it is. In trying to understand the differences, we can't neatly "isolate the variable" of the forms of learning at not-school from school (or vice versa). Secondly, there is very little tracking of individuals through these settings, and so it is difficult to make claims for work on short-term, local projects, which often have variable attendance and participation. Young people may cycle through these settings, have differing experiences of formal schooling, and may repeat or begin anew in different circumstances, and the lack of any long-term studies examining the quality of learning in these centers only compounds the tentative nature of conclusions we might draw about the benefits of learning there.

In some ways it is very difficult to sustain an argument that organized out-of-school constitutes a sector except perhaps in those countries where long-lasting, stable centers with a dedicated professional staff base—such as youth clubs in Germany or forms of "social pedagogy" in Denmark—can meet definitions of consistency and permanence.[3] However, it does seem reasonable to think of what provision young people might encounter as occupying a particular institutional form in the context of their overall learning ecology. By this I mean that if we were to imagine learning experiences from the perspective of an individual, we would see that they encounter types and categories of learning experiences that are framed by providers in certain ways, and that learners make connections between the kinds of learning in formal and non-formal settings.

Focus of the Report

The types of learning prevalent in the not-school sector are the focus of this report. The aim is to explore the work of scholars who have investigated the specific kinds of learning that can be attributed to these not-school experiences.

Much of the literature about this sector has been produced by the sector for funders in the form of evaluations. There does not seem to be a long-standing consistent academic tradition about ways to characterize the qualities of learning in out-of-school settings. The field of study is relatively new. While there are departments of social pedagogy in Scandinavian and German universities that publish long-standing key texts and have a standard academic infrastructure of journals[4] and other kinds of practitioner education, these studies are more wide-ranging than simply about exploring learning—which, as we shall see, isn't always defined as a key objective of the sector.

The social pedagogy tradition isn't as strong in the English-speaking world, where much interest in the field frequently stems from the community of practitioners, policymakers, education experts, and researchers. It has thus tended to focus on how many of these out-of-school centers work—what might be called a supplier-side perspective. Indeed much of the literature explores questions of management, delivery, and implementation. Many evaluations focus only on particular and often short-term projects. Much writing is concerned with improving delivery and particularly in justifying the case for investment in this sector, which inevitably can seem parochial to outsiders. While many studies of school and schooling are often critical and challenging, there is a tradition of many out-of-school providers employing academics to carry out this research to confer authority and status to findings, to facilitate successful advocacy, and to promote these initiatives.

I am in general not casting any aspersions about this mix of aims and practice. Making a case for the value of after-school programs is important, and especially in the context of a general historical shift from a traditional agreement about educational values to analysis of a more technocratic world. However, I want to focus as exclusively as possible on questions about learning and to extrapolate from this mix of studies and analysis only those works that offer a distinctive sense of what kinds of learning can be offered in these not-school settings. Sometimes disentangling this aim from questions about management, delivery, and so forth can be difficult and academically challenging. Nevertheless, I aim to offer a more secure basis upon which future evaluations about learning in these centers can be conceptualized, described, and analyzed.

Why Is This Important?

A key subtheme of this report is to bring a wider international perspective to bear on what often comes across as rather local and introspective studies. It is beyond the scope here to offer a complete global comparison, but, as is suggested above, the tendency in writing about this sector to focus on local or national readerships means that the value of international comparators can be missed, and I would like to introduce at least an element of this wider perspective. I have direct experience of working this sector in the United Kingdom (Sefton-Green 2006) and use examples from the UK, Scandinavia, and the United States.

A second subtheme is to reflect on changes affecting what it means to grow up today and to consider historically what this might mean for the contemporary institutions serving young people. In many countries there is renewed interest in the out-of-school sector and significant policy investment in initiatives. Some of this interest, I will suggest, isn't entirely benign but does stem from a wide range of interest in supporting and coping with young people. Young people are under scrutiny as perhaps never before. The competitive pressure of education seems intense and a concern with learning now dominates discussion of leisure time and everyday family life. This in turn has focused attention on not-school programs and perhaps placed them in the spotlight as being able to carry wider and deeper social functions than originally envisioned. There is increased investment in this sector as a form of supplement to formal education in schools both to remediate their weaknesses and to buttress against other forms of social fracture. Learning in not-schools now has a different level of expectation, which is why we need more analysis to comprehend what might be plausible and possible.

Outline of the Report

This report is not a comprehensive review of the literature or survey of major programs in after-school programs but more of a curated "thematic analysis" of salient principles and landmark studies. Chapters 2 and 3 investigate how the idea of learning has been theorized in not-school environments and enumerate meta-reviews of learning in not-school environments. The aim of these chapters is to ascertain the current state of scholarship about the field to see how and in what ways learning has been described within it.

Chapters 4 through 6 explore three key themes within the literature and, where possible, compare and contrast US with non-US studies to highlight core conceptual issues as well as to help us identify what we tend to take for granted. Chapter 4 examines studies of creative media production. Chapter 5 explores the idea of metalearning and learning-to-learn revolving around analyses of language and technology. Chapter 6 attempts to identify more traditionally disciplined forms of informal learning—that is, learning pursued in the home during leisure time—and see how those experiences and that understanding is developed in not-school surroundings.

The conclusion draws together themes from the discussion, ending with an agenda for future research in this area.

2 Understanding Learning in Not-School Environments

This chapter outlines some of the different ways that the idea of learning has been theorized in not-school environments and offers up some questions about what might constitute the key dimensions of learning theories at work in the day-to-day transactions that go on in such places. Of course, the idea of learning itself is vast and encompassing: on one level, by interrogating how learning might be different in these locations, we open the door to trying to understand what learning might mean in the abstract. This is a huge and complex task beyond the scope of this report. However, whereas in the previous chapter we saw how commonsense assumptions about what happens in schools dominates our uses of words such as "education" or "learning," here we need to explore what might be the everyday or quotidian ways that we might conceptualize out-of-school learning.

Hyphens and Plurals

A common and popular way to describe non-school learning is to use a series of hyphenated phrases like non-formal or in-formal learning. This echoes a tendency in current discourse to expand what was once considered singular—as in media literacy, information literacy, or computer literacy, and so-on.

However, the terms in- and non-formal learning aren't in themselves straightforward or easy to define. Are we talking about the quality of the learning—the nature of *what* is learned—or its context—*where* the learning takes place? Or the pedagogic process at work within learning transactions—*how* the learning takes place in practice? What indeed might be the relationship between degrees of formality from the learner's point of view, and how might experiences from formal and non-formal contexts relate to each other?

In general,[5] discussion often focuses on the question of explicit curriculum structure: how the learning is framed and by whom (the learner or other kinds of teachers)? In addition, the research has focused on how notions of achievement or attainment are regulated—how do learners know they have learned something? How this is measured and by whom?

Many discussions of curriculum structure aren't focused on the intrinsic (how knowledge might be organized "inside people's heads" or deployed in specific contexts) but look to the extrinsic—that is, showing how such knowledge (or capability or skill) might be packaged or organized for its transmission. This again reinforces an attention to the traditional ways in which we have carved up histories of knowledge and bodies of understanding. Non- and in-formal learning(s) are defined by the degree they vary from the norms derived from the common sense of schooling. The literature has thus developed a continuum for degrees of formality. An OECD publication (Werquin

2010) builds on a convention developed in the European Union and common in much European literature, providing a tripartite model of definition.

As Werquin summarizes, *formal learning* (typically) happens in public school systems and leads to widely accepted forms of credentials (although we know that much learning within such institutions takes place in-formally). The *non-formal* learning sector describes a wide range of institutions usually funded privately (or if funded by the public, they may not be statutory) and dedicated to a wide range of activities and disciplines, where the curriculum might follow some structure, plan, or pattern but usually will not lead to credentials. The non-formal sector by definition includes a broad range of practices that can be taught and learned but may not figure in the narrow formal curriculum we are used to. Of course, teaching and learning within this sector may be highly organized and "formal." By definition, the voluntary nature of participation sets up different expectations among teachers and their charges as well as framing the power relationships in classrooms or workshops in ways that are different from school. Work-based learning comes into this category.

Finally, *in-formal learning* describes individualized study undertaken at the learner's own speed and driven by the learner. In that sense both the formal and non-formal imply a notion of curriculum—of an order, plan, and structure unfolding and of development—whereas here in-formal learning suggests that such knowledge is framed more by the agency and direction of the learner than by the social practices usually employed in teaching. Again, learners can follow set courses by themselves,

and in all three cases, it is easy to think of exceptions and challenges to this framework. Nevertheless, this model and these
kinds of definitions do seem to capture key points of difference
in how learning is understood and organized: and continuing to
use such terms does consolidate such ideas as describing firm
social truths.

There is a considerable critical literature exploring these ideas
(Bekerman, Burbules, Keller, and Silberman-Keller 2005; Coffield 2000; Drotner, Jensen, and Schroder 2009). While virtually
no scholars are terribly concerned about defining these terms in
watertight and exclusive ways, acknowledging that ideas are at
best relational (understood in relation to what they are not)
rather than absolute, there is a commitment to exploring and
analyzing other kinds of learning than only that which happens
in schools. There is, additionally, an explicitly political use to
these terms, suggesting that because they challenge the status
quo and broaden our understanding of learning in the abstract,
they add useful concepts to the public domain. Furthermore,
there is an accepted point of view that this kind of analysis
offers an important kind of social "recognition." This in turn,
"provides greater visibility and therefore potential value to the
learning outcomes and the competences of people in the labor
market" (Werquin 2010).

However, this raises a strange reflexive anxiety in that it is
acknowledged that as scholars research, describe, analyze, and
categorize varieties of in-formal and non-formal learning, they
in effect formalize that learning and thus run the risk of destroying the very quality of difference that distinguishes non- and
in-formal learning from their inverse. This academic concern is

mirrored in the administrative and policy uses of the not-school sector—the more we develop complex programs out of school, the more we have to face the challenge of not turning not-schools into schools. Visibility and recognition are double-edged kinds of affirmation, and we will return to this conundrum throughout the rest of our discussion.

While some ideas will return in discussion of texts about not-school learning experiences in chapters 4 through 6, the rest of this chapter will expand key concepts underpinning these formulations.

1 Context

Historically the study of in-formal and non-formal learning is tied to understanding the role of place. Scholarship about non-formal learning in developing non-Western countries—from which some of the first uses of the term came—was often focused on supporting alternative sites of learning than (in these cases) problematic and underdeveloped school systems.[6] Scholars of the workplace were also interested in how work-related knowledge and work-related processes of collaboration or hierarchy determined both how people learned to become workers as well as how companies could maximize the skills of their workforce. In the literature from both of these traditions, place is more than just an empty and neutral space, and its social particularity has always been important to the discussion (Edwards 2009).

The idea of context encompasses many of these elements, and contemporary scholarship is also interested in how the dimensions of context affect or perhaps even constitute learning

(Edwards, 2009; Edwards, Biesta, and Thorpe 2009; Schegloff 1997). Context is more than just where the learning takes place. While social geography remains important, especially, for instance, in thinking about where not-schools are places in the community, the kinds of buildings they take place in, and the design of spaces for learning in both customized buildings or indeed where projects "squat" in mixed-use facilities, there is even more to this important idea. In essence, context encompasses the set of relationships—visible, invisible, inherited, and assumed—in which the social interactions of the learning take place.

Non-formal and in-formal learning tend to take place in contexts where teaching and learning aren't usually understood to be the primary purposes of place—in contradistinction to a school. However, the expectations of a setting and especially the orientation and behaviors of other participants are vital to a full appreciation of context. Other participants can also include tools or equipment, which can be characterized as being physical or even as abstract as language and other kinds of semiotic resources. The sociocultural tradition has long paid attention to the power of meditational means—that is, a focus on objects or semiotic process (forms of meaning making) that offer particular affordances in social situations (Wertsch 1997). For example, when we use certain kinds of tools (from a simple hammer to a complex computer), the tools make certain kinds of meaning making possible and limit others. One key role of *technology* in learning derives from this perspective, and there are many studies of how certain kinds of technologies offer very particular kinds of opportunities for learning in specific settings from

Xerox engineers to computers to weaving. The ways that technologies allow us to escape the limits of face-to-face interactions, initially though forms of distance learning in dispersed societies like Canada or Australia, and now through various kinds of Web-based technologies, additionally allows us to play with the suspension of time as well as of space in educational transactions.

Settings, participants, and tools are also considered across time, so the idea of context can also encompass expectations, prior experiences, and the orientations and trajectories people bring with them and take away from specific interactions. Here studies of professionals, values, the embedding of practices in social interactions, and kinds of communities of practice offer valuable insight for educators (Wenger 1999). In this tradition, exploring how people are inducted into long-standing ways of behaving is another way in which learning is conceptualized and framed (Lave and Wenger 1991).

A particular subtheme in this approach is where context is taken to include the habits and traditions associated with particular kinds of practice, from the theater to fast food outlets to high finance (Holland, Skinner, and Cain 1998). The disciplinary practices associated with various kinds of endeavors are often key to understanding the learning going on, as in studies of people working in the theater as performers, where how you behave, what language you use, and how you model yourself on more experienced practitioners are all examples of a kind of learning that is inseparable from its context (Felstead et al. 2007).

As in the next two sections, it should be acknowledged that there is nothing in principle that differentiates the use of context in learning in non-formal learning from that taking place in schools. However, studies of learning in non-formal domains almost always draw attention to the specificities of context because it is so crucial in helping us understand the different ways that learners are absorbing information or being socialized, in learning to behave, to imitate, and to be initiated into practice. It is striking how learning is so often not considered in these ways in the literature about school and schooling because we tend to take the practice, the everyday of schooling, for granted rather than see it as a singularity among others in ways that the not-school tradition allow us to do.

2   The Learner

The second key dimension of in-formal and non-formal learning is the learner. One evident feature of many studies of learners in school is, of course, an attention to the developmental perspective: how children change as they grow older, what patterns of growth they exhibit, what norms we establish for cohorts. In turn, this kind of approach affects how we imagine children's lives in general, and much parenting focuses on these questions—not only on, for example, babies as they grow and begin to talk or when young children learn to read, but also as a way of explaining living with adolescents. Very little of this developmentalist perspective is present in how we conceptualize learning in not-schools except as we import it from the school literature and our expectations. As we will see in the next chapter, there are very few studies of learning at not-school that borrow either the experimental or even the psychological paradigm to make sense of not-school experiences, and we know very little about how young people might circulate through not-school settings as well as how such experience informs school, home, and other learning. The supplier interest we have already noted also means that the important distinctions between provision for youth (often in the United States described as community-based) is not the same as after-school activities often aimed at younger children.

However, the learner in not-school settings is theorized in two important ways: in respect of their interest, enthusiasm, and motivation, and along an a emotional axis in terms of their relationships with others, especially adults. The former focus in a sense posits the figure of the learner as possessing agency and individual choice that is frequently denied in other settings. Yet the latter focus is often preoccupied with deficits, with the absence of parenting figures in young people's lives and the needs of the young for support and security.

The idea of interest and motivation by learners is significantly concerned with its opposite, the negative proposition—how to deal with people who know what they don't like. The figure of the alienated unmotivated recusant certainly inhabits the literature of school (in)effectiveness. Besides the obvious issue about trying to deal with de- and un-motivated learners, motivation is crucial to how we understand the whole process because learning is often characterized by its deliberative and intentional nature (Varenne 2007). It is usually acknowledged that motivations (whether emotional, strategic, or tactical) are necessary in this sense to achieve a state of intention and orientation to learning (Boekaerts 2010).

Interest isn't the same thing as motivation and is often used to suggest preferences across domains of activity. In some respects it might be helpful to think of *interest* and *motivation* as weak terms that we use to describe strong concepts. They go very deep into notions of human nature and our everyday conceptions of our own and others' lives; but they are elusive. Both concepts are central to the idea of non-formal and informal learning, and in many cases the not-school sectors are built on the assumption that they (not school) offer a greater degree of interest-led learning experiences, generating more motivation, it could be said, than is commonly found in many schools.

In the same way, learning in the non-formal sectors is frequently characterized by a high degree of affect, not just in the investment made by learners in their own experiences, but also where interacting with teachers and other kinds of mentor and authority figures is part of the learning involved. Given the importance of context, the transactions in not-schools are often as much valued for their psychosocial impacts—the effect on the personhood of the learner—as on the content of the transactions. Again the same is also true for schools, but it is notable how the literature about learning in not-schools explicitly and frequently emphasizes this relationship dynamic as being central to the figure of the learner.

3   Knowledge

From this perspective it might seem that at times non-formal learning is contentless, that it is about process or developing the learner, but that would be a premature conclusion. As we will see in later chapters, in some cases, learning is conceptualized at a metalevel as being about learning or the learner (chapter 5), but in many other examples, content is king. However, the not-school lens does allow both for the definition of other kinds of knowledge as well as finding ways of disciplinary knowledge to be transformed in non-school settings.

A key insight from studies of work-based learning is that in practice, implicit and tacit forms of understanding are as central to the performance of many activities as the explicit demonstration of achievement we are used to from a test-based school system (Eraut 1994). What counts as knowledge is often hidden or embodied—it is enacted in the doing—rather than a question of the manipulation of symbolic languages, as is so often the case in school tests.

Not only is this kind of knowledge part of the non-formal repertoire of learning but also other less-sanctioned domains than the constrained school curriculum also find their place in not-school settings. This includes various practices that possess all the qualities of formal knowledge domains (erudition, arcane mastery, canonical texts, and scholarly tradition) but which— such as comic fandom—are socially marginalized for many reasons.[7] Knowledge in our society is not, and should not be, restricted to formal education; the non-formal sector is full of activities that we value socially and that are structured in terms of mastery and knowledge but are rarely found in the school curriculum. The boundaries between socially sanctioned forms of knowledge and skills and schooled knowledge are constantly shifting, however, and practices such as graffiti or street dance, for instance, which once may once have been the preserve of the non-formal are now found in well-respected art galleries and dance troupes.

This idea of there being uncredited secondary-knowledge domains that make equivalent demands on the acquisition of knowledge and skills—indeed, on forms of specialized learning to the school curriculum—is central to the idea of non-formal learning. Different countries and regions have different traditions of valuing the totality of social practices, and the diversity of human experience means anyway that often it is for pragmatic or economic reasons that certain knowledge domains are included or excluded within the school system. Comparative studies of, for example, theater and drama show how this kind of knowledge, usually not perceived as controversial, nevertheless is differentially available within the formal learning sector (DICE Consortium 2010).

Other formations of noncurricularized knowledge derive from ideas as diverse and everyday as common sense to street smarts (T. McLaughlin 1996). British cultural theorists such as Paul Willis are likely to characterize knowledge domains in cultural terms as in his analysis of "symbolic creativity" (Willis 1990) or as a form of social semiotics (Hodge and Kress 2007), local knowledge (Geertz 1985), professionalization (Freidson 2001), or even the social life of information, (Brown and Duguid 2000). All of these studies highlight challenges to the categorization and changing value of differential knowledge domains. This then necessitates a concomitant reevaluation of what it means to be an educated person subject to these different forms of measurement and value (Levinson, Foley, and Holland 1996).

Summary

This chapter has attempted to map out the different dimensions of in-formal and non-formal learning. The literature has explored key aspects of context, looking at location, participants, and their orientations, and technologies at the same time as reconceptualizing the learners as possessing agency, intention, and feeling. Equally, what we mean by knowledge—how it is arranged, regulated, and controlled, and even its intrinsic characteristics—are now applied across a range of social domains that grow ever more complex in the day-to-day of contemporary social change. I have suggested that none of this is exclusive to what I have called the *not-school sector* but that the literature drives analysis forward with a new intensity and sense of purpose.

3   Researching Not-School

This chapter explores those reviews of the non-formal learning sector that relate to young people (that is, excluding broad community-oriented, adult, and workplace-directed studies). The aim of the chapter is to ascertain the current state of scholarship about the field, to see how learning has been described within it. In general, I shall be looking at more metalevel and broad-ranging reports: detailed accounts of specific institutions and projects will be found in subsequent chapters.

Four important methodological challenges within this field of study influence the quality, range, and depth of scholarship.

1. Data Scarcity   Although we will see some accounts of activity, there are very few accounts of investment and performance at the local, regional, and national levels. To my knowledge, we cannot compare, for example, attendance, consistency of programs, or even core purposes across countries. Even within countries it is difficult to find accurate data on basic facts such as the spread of provision. The Scandinavian countries and Germany do have well-established youth-work sectors financed by the State; these traditions have influenced a degree of cross-country information and analysis at the level of the European union.[8] Nevertheless, even in those countries with developed youth sectors,[9] it is difficult to claim the level of insight into questions of funding, programs, participation, and so on that we associate with formal education systems.

Within interest-led initiatives—drama or art for young people are good examples—there is often more consistent comparison; see, for example, (Bamford 2006; DICE Consortium 2010). This is partly because there are communities of practitioners in these sorts of subsectors and because variance in institutional form and shape doesn't hinder how professional practitioners identify with the sector (DICE Consortium 2010).

2. Equity Issues Many kinds of after-school programs both for children and youth are not free at point of entry. They can be exclusive and expensive, although much provision is subsidized and low cost. Studies of the sector generally do not explore private programs. Sociologists of childhood have paid much attention to extracurricular learning in relatively affluent middle-class homes, in families striving to develop young people as social and cultural capital (Lareau 2003; Pugh 2009). One key implication for us from this literature is how partaking in these exclusive enrichment activities can end up making certain kinds of knowledge and experiences available only to sections of the population. The remediation work that many funders of the sector aspire to is geared toward broadening the knowledge base of populations with limited financial resources.

3. Traversals Jay Lemke's insights into the ways in which learning occurs across moments, timescales, and place have a particular resonance at a practical level for us (Lemke 2000; 2008). Not only is participation voluntary and therefore can vary in intensity, duration, and by implication, effect; but also we have virtually no research exploring how young people participate in not-school in the context of other life experiences. Rare even within ethnographic accounts of children or youth is any sense of how participation in not-school relates to other kinds of participation patterns. Again, the fact that, generally, young people are at school for fixed periods of their lives—for only about six hours per day and during a limited time in their life span—means that not-school experiences, which are long-term, tend to be extrapolated as a form of unfair comparison. A rare exception to this is Mike Ashley's retrospective study of grown-up male dancers—young men he had worked with on a community-based dance project (Ashley 2009).

4. Politics and Advocacy Although all research is biased in some way, studies about not-school seem especially open to the accusation that they are partial. Much of the research is funded by the implementers themselves (this is as true for government-funded projects as for privately funded ones), and there is a high preponderance of project evaluations—which of course find it difficult to ask and answer the bigger questions about learning and life-course trajectories. Evaluations tend to address questions of effectiveness and impact within the conceptual framework of an initiative, which can restrict investigation of wider issues. Finally, as already noted because not-school is expensive and regarded as an extra rather than core (again, this is true only in certain countries), advocates often feel the need to over-claim and to justify effectiveness as part of the advocacy function within research, which can create a further set of problems and inhibit coming to a greater understanding of learning.

Do Reviews of Work in the Sector Offer Us a Typology of Learning?

The Sociocultural Approach

A relatively recent review of research in education published by the American Research Education Association, and therefore aimed at an academic review of field, attempted to map learning in in-formal contexts—those not designed for the formal demands of schooling—suggesting that there was a very broad literature base examining learning in informal contexts (Vadeboncoeur 2006). On the other hand, it is a common lament in much of the literature that the field is insufficiently theorized (Hirsch 2005). Jennifer Vadeboncoeur describes a systematic process of exploring possible ways of categorizing and sorting accounts of practice, project descriptions, and academic studies. She traces a history through the various constructions of formal, in-formal, and non-formal education, as described in the previous chapter, concluding that the sociocultural frame that understands learning not as happening through an individualistic or cognitive process but "as realized through participation in everyday social practices" (2006, 247) allows us to synthesize possible contradictions.

She writes, "I would argue that learning always occurs in context and that contexts define what counts as learning," leading to the suggestion that "what is needed is an approach to identifying and describing a context, or a *participation framework* for mapping the context of learning. . . . Articulating a general participation framework may be one way to study how contexts for learning in general are constituted and sustained" (247–248, italics added). This further develops the general position about the role of context in learning explained in the previous chapter.

She then offers case studies of learning in communities of practice within the performing arts; programs that foster science, literacy, or technology exploration; and museums and science centers. She further develops five key dimensions of context: location, relationships, content, pedagogy, and assessment. The aim therefore in this approach is not so much to fetishize non- or in-formal learning but investigate "how . . . a particular context contribute[s] to learning?" (272).

This commitment to the sociocultural frame is important. Vadeboncoeur essentially argues that holding on to the sector as an organizational concept is not a productive way to help us focus on questions of learning because that in and of itself it is never likely to be a significant determinant of a learning context. In that sense, I speculate that she might say that the idea of not-school is on one level a conceptual distraction. Her work is important and lays out very clearly a model of learning. It is one of the most elaborate metastudies of the field and focuses on learning rather than on the supplier-side issues raised in chapter 1. The notion of a "participation framework" is generative, and we will return to it later in this report.

I want to offer two kinds of challenges to Vadeboncoeur's argument. The first relates to the question of the researchers' perspective and the second to the conceptual difficulty of characterizing interpersonal and identity-based learning.

Vadeboncoeur's three main areas of study present us with a chicken-and-egg problem, which comes down to how scholars impose interpretative perspectives on social phenomena. In this instance, each of her three main sections relies on preexisting ideas about what constitutes learning. Literacy, science, and technology initiatives are all predicated on translating schooled understandings of those domains into not-school environments. The same is true of the learning in museums and science centers—which are clearly part of society's educational institutions, if technically not part of school. Even the application of communities of practice to performing-arts projects is based on the application of theoretical concepts to these practices, however recognized that there is considerable tradition of understanding not-school performing arts in this way.

This is a genuinely baffling intellectual conundrum: Latour describes this as using the social to understand the social (Latour 2007). In this context, the question is whether we are using ideas about learning to describe and analyze what we observe, not, as is often the case in scientific understanding, the other way around. Can we ever escape our preconceptions of learning or do we just impose them? In another wide-ranging review of not-school experiences, Sara Hill uses the metaphor "cookie cutter" to describe how the contributors to her volume structure their case studies around these common frames: "theoretical understanding," "program content and design," "academic standards," "youth development" and "replication in other contexts" (Hill 2007). Hill's solution to our conceptual dilemma is to deliberately use the discourse of educationalists and education professionals to extrapolate from her wide-ranging scenarios a common core. Hill, however, does acknowledge that this logic runs the risk of effacing the difference she wants to highlight.

This too is the problem with the second challenge to Vadeboncoeur's approach: the extent to which a sociocultural framework can capture questions about aspects of identity and the intrapersonal dimensions of participation. The sociocultural approach tends to be suspicious of attempts to psychologize, to individualize, and even to describe learning in cognitivist terms, preferring to argue that meaning is socially constructed, including concepts of the self. As a consequence, the language of affect and ways of capturing the inter- and intrapersonal are to an extent neglected in this literature. Vadeboncoeur makes it clear that she is interested in questions about relationships. Other important metalevel studies of the field, however, such as those by Barton Hirsch and Milbrey McLaughlin, strive hard to capture these qualities and suggest that they are central to the nature of the learning going on in our field (Hirsch 2005; M. W. McLaughlin 1999; M. W. McLaughlin et al. 2009; M. McLaughlin, Irby, and Langman 1994).

Personal Development and Learning

As we noted in the section about the learner in the last chapter, ideas about personal development and changing subjectivities are important to notions of learning in this sector. Many projects have explicit goals of affecting the learner both individually and as a member of a community. The difficulty, however, is how to define these complex and value-laden notions of inter- or intra-subjective change and growth without defaulting to a discourse of developmentalism (a normative model of what we might expect at different ages) or a discourse of deficit (the idea that young people from nonwhite, middle-class homes are lacking so-called normal social attributes).

These are considerable challenges, and as a society we don't find it easy to talk about such things: the language of the sociocultural landscape is in some ways safer. It is precisely at this difficult intersection of deficit discourse and personal change, however, that important scholars locate the nature of the learning in our sector (M. McLaughlin et al. 1994). In subsequent research, for example, M. W. McLaughlin and her colleagues (2009) use methods of long-term ethnographic observation, including extensive interviews, to get a feel for how social interactions change people. Her work not only stresses the power of individual agency for change (that is, how the learner might develop) but also the importance of individuals who can facilitate change in others (that is, how interpersonal interactions affect and change youth). The aim in this tradition of study is get an empirical handle on what it means to talk about viable futures without lapsing into aspiration and thus to understand learning for personal and community transformation.

In these studies, the focus isn't so much on a language of learning but on a process of change. McLaughlin talks about "love and commitment" (38), about forms of identity as learning and learning as identity work about "taking on personal responsibility and self-respect" (M. McLaughlin, Irby, and Langman. 1994, 16). The book characterizes how individuals within youth organizations effect change over others through role modeling, through exemplifying personal discipline, through certain uses of language, and finally through forms of "supportive intimacy" (84). The book emphasizes family relationships, a strong emotional investments in "my kids" (97) and belief that the quality of the interpersonal to an extent trumps decontextualized pedagogy (130). Kinds of local knowledge are more important than abstract claims about hypothetical employability (133–138). An attention to frequency and familiarity in the rhythm of daily life is promoted as central to developing habits of change.

Urban Sanctuaries (McLaughlin, Irby, and Langman 1994) has established standards from which subsequent interpretations can be developed. It has also set a standard for looking at learning as a narrative of change and the place of the personal, where special persons (McLaughlin calls them "wizards") are central actors within these narratives. The "it" that wizards know how to do is not a model program but rather a community created by adults associated with the program who respect the attitudes, interests, and the needs of the youth themselves (218).

A key methodological concern is that "programs should not be studied in isolation from the features that [are] meaningful to youth" (4). In some ways a focus on learning might fall afoul of this prescription. Certainly, a more recent study of the sector from this broad tradition takes that view (Hirsch 2005). Hirsch is more interested in the quality of the teaching or other modes of alternative pedagogy in not-school as opposed to the content or the facts of "educational" transactions (Hirsch 2005, 125). His argument is that "relationships between youth and staff are the heart and soul . . . of after-school programs," thus relegating the importance of "structured programming" to second place (131). This approach builds on work by Rhodes, showing how mentoring and relationship qualities are key to change, which is how such advocates define learning in these contexts (Rhodes 2004). In this analysis, learning is not imagined in ways that can unshackle it from its formulations with schooling, and thus, as Hirsch notes, as we don't want to make urban communities like schools, it seems counterproductive to pursue a narrow learning agenda. The learning he sees as being characteristic of the sector is moral, disciplined, inter- and intrasubjective, and thus about a form of being in a social context. This he is reluctant to sacrifice to other outcomes often wished on after-school programs, especially those concerned with narrow performance-related ends.

Instead, Hirsch prefers to offer a general model of learning as a capacity to learn—that is, learning to learn. In this formulation, Hirsch eschews learning as defined as the acquisition of specific content in favor of a broad disposition and an orientation to learning itself. Although there aren't enough studies exploring more analytically what this might mean, there is a tendency here to construct learning to learn in psychosocial terms, in terms of habits and dispositions.[10]

Summary

In the previous chapter, we explored how, in general, learning in not-school has been conceptualized across three key theoretical domains: context, the learner, and knowledge. In this chapter, we have seen that key meta-reviews of practice in the sector—those focusing on questions of learning—demonstrate that these concepts have coalesced around sociocultural approaches and those that emphasize development as more person-centered.

We have also noted how our studies over a twenty-five-year period indicate some interesting historical trends in emphasis and approach. The first relates to the tendency noted in the studies by McLaughlin et al. and Hirsch of a different kind of emphasis on the individual as opposed to the community as the object of intervention; secondly, as observed in Hirsch's work we can see the emergence of a debate around the instrumentalization of learning in after-school with a tendency to emphasize other outcomes than social values—especially when those seem more interested in producing workers than citizens. Finally, as hinted at by Vadeboncoeur, the tendency to turn more and more of everyday life into an educational opportunity—that is, the spread of a moral surveillance, so that dimensions of what used to be a private and unknown in everyday life by children is now deemed appropriate for turning into an educational experience.

The next three chapters will focus in more detail on individual studies in each chapter that explore how these trends over time are also changing how we think about the learning itself. Where possible, I will try to compare and contrast US with non-US studies to highlight conceptual issues, as well as to help us identify what we take for granted what can be seen as particular to a time and place.

4   Culture and Identity: Creative Media Production

In this chapter and chapters 5 and 6, we will concentrate on comparing some key studies from this field. As I explained in the introduction, this is not a comprehensive literature review but more a "curated" thematic analysis. I have selected three key themes for further analysis. This is partly suggested by the literature, what in my view constituted high-quality and lasting studies in what is not always a field with common standards, and partly by the key themes emerging from previous chapters. As noted at the last chapter, I aimed to contrast studies from different countries (traditions) and times to make explicit trends and values.

This chapter focuses on the theme of creative media production: that is, studies of youth (broadly speaking, 14 to 25, rather than children) who are engaged in structured creative activities, where they are involved in making forms of popular media, broadcasting, photography, or film. The media aspect is only one side of the coin, as the studies of these projects were interested in questions about cultural identity—that is, how learning to make forms of media also relates to notions of the self as socially positioned (Halverson 2010). Both key studies—the first by Andrew Dewdney and Martin Lister, the second by Elisabeth Soep and Vivian Chávez—try to situate their educational activities in a wider sociopolitical analysis of youth, especially minority youth, and extended forms of creative identity work. The projects, described in both studies are however, reflective and genuinely inquiring about what this tenet of faith in the youth sector means in practice. It is this fusion of topic and self that creates the *participation framework*, in Vadeboncoeur's terms, which connects the studies described here.

England in the 1980s: *Youth, Culture, and Photography*

The then-unitary education authority for London in the early 1980s ran the Cockpit Arts Centre, which offered a mixture of after-school, out-of-school, and vacation programs for young people as well as developed programs for teacher education. In 1988 two of the workers in the Department of Cultural Studies published *Youth, Culture, and Photography* (Dewdney and Lister 1988). This book is a substantial and detailed account of a series of programs they ran between 1979 and 1985. It is interesting for us because it has a clear and distinct theory of learning and a set of educational practices for and by young people marking out forms of community-based not-school experiences. It contains a significant amount of photographs by young people in various programs, which are analyzed at length.

The key to Dewdney and Lister's (1988) theory of learning drew on then-recent work in British Cultural Studies and, in particular, theories of resistance, style, and identity. The central argument of the book is that forms of creative expression, primarily aspects of photography (including both documentary and constructed work) both draws on and constitutes key processes of identification as classed, gendered, and racialized subjectivity. This means paying attention to the ways we all mark membership of, or difference from, social groups around us. Because it is self-evidently a signifying practice, photography is particularly acute at focusing on how we signal this process though "manner of speech, physical posture, gesture, appearance, ways of relating or not relating to others, ways of ordering, prioritising how time is spent, and attention to the context and location of these actions" (29). This ensemble of choice adds up to what they call the "practice of style. A style then is a considered and related set of signifying, culturally located practices" (29). Style is how working-class youth in particular express ideas through forms of resistance against dominant subject positions.

Youth, Culture, and Photography then describes both a set of curriculum activities and analyses of work made by young people in these programs to illustrate a progressive way of supporting reflection, skills acquisition, and development, and a critical reception to photography. It starts out talking about portraits, then about interest-driven locations, studies of self and context, printing, development of text to go with images, and finally a discussion about the status of photography in domestic and art cultures. It concludes with observations about the collective and social uses of photography, how style supports and develops group reflexivity and identity, and speculates about how these perspectives foster understanding of growth into adulthood. It argues that we all need to take this work seriously, that it represents social, cultural, gendered, and classed modes of being that give it larger existential value beyond simply being something for kids to learn about; that it documents and gives insight into deep social process of interest to all. The idea of engaging with resistance (101) both validates young people as well as possibly contributes to future employability by enabling a work with the self. Unlike contemporary accounts of creative practices, however, how photography might become a consistent social practice, as a hobby in adult life, is also advocated. The transferability of critical and creative skills to other later-in-life types of education is a key part of the learning identified in these programs.

Aspects of this argument will be familiar to readers, although I am also highlighting key differences and without the host of images in the book it is difficult to do justice to the subtlety of the analysis. One of my favorite examples is "the youth albums" produced as part of "weekend assignments" made by mid-teen-aged people; they made interest-led montages of symbolically important images from their homes. I have revisited this text because I suggest it is interesting for four specific reasons.

• Although working with excluded and minority youth who are often in difficult and challenging communities, the projects in this this report start from the premise that the young people's behaviors are not in any way lacking or in need of remediation but in and of themselves demonstrate rational and coherent creative responses to experience. Introducing a critical reflective dimension into this process is where learning starts. By situating identity work at the heart of the interventions and by characterizing the process of identity as "work" and as a set of semiotic processes, it opens the door for both a subjective and a social effect. This self-centeredness is not the same starting point as a psychologistic model of interest because it suggests that the "stuff" of the learner can be worked on in these kinds of practices outside of school.

• The programs are interesting because of their relationship with school and schooled learning. This works at a number of levels. On the one hand, the book advocates a form of organized progressive (in the sense of developing curriculum) study that looks in many ways like a school curriculum, and at times the authors discuss the similarities between work in school to the activity in their program. On the other hand, they suggest that school simply is a too constraining and problematic locus for this kind of work and that questions about identity are too challenging to realistically find a place at school. In other words, not-school provides a unique kind of social space for the formal exploration of personally meaningful concepts.

• Even at the time photography was not a new subject, even if a slightly unorthodox one, and another interesting point of relationship with school is how the formal curriculum knowledge at this point in time in a subject's disciplinary trajectory actually finds greater purchase outside the school. This is an interesting point of reference for the host of courses in new media that have emerged in recent years outside of schools but which, as this report suggests, will find their way through a gradual process of what can be termed *curricularization* into the subject-discipline framework that we associate with schooled knowledge.

• Recuperating subjects into the academic curriculum, however, is only part of the process of familiarization suggested by

Dewdney and Lister, as they suggest that a key impact of this work will not be at the level of transferable skills or credentials but offering a level of personal and political fulfillment. Here the wider of project of the book finds a new way to reconfigure the relationships between home and school. The community basis of the not-school here works only because it offers space for the domestic and the home culture to be reconfigured and acknowledged.[11] The re-working with these technologies can either lead back into the home—as a way of enhancing every-day cultural practice—or back into the academy. Again, we are familiar with this interplay of new media technologies at home, school, and the wider culture. *Youth, Culture and Photography*, I suggest, sets down a marker in how forms of disciplined cultural work take place across these hitherto discrete domains and yet requires an intermediate space for learning, experimentation, validation, and curriculum development.

Oakland in the Twenty-First Century: Youth Radio

While the Cockpit Arts Centre was funded by local government, the site for Elisabeth Soep and Vivian Chávez's study, the Youth Radio project in Oakland, California, is funded by a mixture of philanthropic grants and operates as a non-profit organization (Soep and Chávez 2010). As its name suggests, the organization works with young people to create radio programs. In the United States, programs are broadcast locally and sometimes franchised nationally. Of course, digital convergence now means that radio can now include other media, Web pages, and images, along with audio. Like Dewdney and Lister, Soep and

Chávez offer a study of production and learning in which organized curricula, learning progression, and youth output all intersect in their analysis. Their work is built around the study of young people's (mainly late teens to early twenties) creative productions. The authors offer us transcribed text of finished output and additional ethnographic accounts from within episodes, but like Dewdney and Lister, they place much stress on reproducing the output of young people and making the case that it is of value in and of itself as well as for what it tells us about learning.

Like Dewdney and Lister, participants are to an extent self-selected, participation is voluntary, albeit both sets of programs start with a larger pool of students than those completing production at the end, implying a staged model of participation. Soep and Chávez argue that the work of youth radio—collective forms of media production as a result of stepped induction activities—offers three distinct kinds of learning: *converged literacy*, *collegial pedagogy*, and *point of voice* (16). In some ways these are both learning processes as well as learning aims. The key point of connection between the Cockpit Centre and Youth Radio is the argument that young people's forms of creative and journalistic expression can belong properly in the public domain (with ownership rights) rather than existing simply as educational output—on the way to becoming something else. Soep and Chávez talk about "draw[ing] and leverag[ing] public interest" or "claim[ing] and exerc[ising] the right to use the media" (46–47) and of how putting production into the public domain raises questions of "public accountability" (69) in these instances both from and about the young producer. The argument here is that this feature of the pedagogy—how production-based curricula work—operates on three levels simultaneously: respecting the social and political agency of youth; and as a consequence, creating a qualitatively different regimen for learning through enhancing both investment in and responsibility toward audience and the effect of the producers' actions; and finally offering a viable alternative to the more simulated curriculum experience in formal schooling.

Both books pay attention to how this variance in role fundamentally restructures the learning, suggesting that reconfiguring the power relations between teacher and pupil is central to the not-school experience. Soep and Chávez coin the phrase *collegial pedagogy* to characterize this dimension in greater detail, exploring what they call *collaborative framing* and *youth-led enquiry* (57). They describe conversations from the Youth Radio production cycle and offer transcripts from broadcast interviews, such as a study of Military Marriage and how that story was negotiated with the show's producer (57–62). They pay great attention to the social relationships that frame the learning experience, suggesting that these interpersonal relationships contribute profoundly to the differences such practices offer. Yet, in line with the best of the studies of youth production, they are cautious and skeptical about a naive faith in youth voice. However much, like Dewdney and Lister, they suggest a reconfiguration of authority and a rebalancing of student participation, this does not mean that everything students do or say is in and of itself always worthy of uncritical celebration. Soep and Chávez's play on words in their discussion of "point of voice" offers a critique of lazy assumptions: that expression in and of itself turns things around for youth (86); that youth by their very nature speak in authentic counternarrative (90); and that the proliferation of digital outlets means never having to compromise (95).

This balancing act between advocating a reconfiguration of authority relationships in pedagogy and yet clearly investigating the difference such rearranging actually makes to the learning is central for a measured appreciation of how these forms of learning work in practice. Soep and Chávez's final insight into learning, like Dewdney and Lister, explores how the kind of knowledge produced in not-school sites can itself lead to curriculum innovation, Whereas Dewdney and Lister were interested in arts practice, Soep and Chávez make a case for what they call *converged literacies*. Their exploration of young people's actual productions reveals an attention to forms of creative rule breaking and to how texts make and remake a greater range of demotic conventions than usually found in formal schooling. Where "authors" are sanctioned in not-school and can experiment means that different paradigms of literacy can be used in these contexts with greater freedom. This idea of converged literacies draws on theories in both media convergence (Jenkins 2006) and new literacy studies (Knobel, Lankshear, and Bigum 2007), thus situates the practice of Youth Radio as an innovative, R&D-like curriculum that explores these new interconnections. This connects with the arguments advanced at the end of the section on *Youth, Culture, and Photography* above. Both studies offer new ways of working in new media forms, developing practices from mainstream media and cultural activity as educational projects.

Unlike Dewdney and Lister, Soep and Chávez are interested in the trajectories of individuals passing through Youth Radio and include a series of biographical narratives that explore an intimate level of change and experience while working at Youth Radio. Like the life histories in work with adults, (for example, Goodson and Sikes 2001) that explore the place and meaning of educational experience in the formation of the self, the case studies in the book add up to a model of individual life-wide learning routes and significant learning episodes. This kind of approach offers a way of reflecting on the larger meaning of the place of not-school experience as rationalized through more mature reflection. The interpersonal dimension of learning in these sites is of prime importance in producing a learning self as the object and subject of these intervention programs. It is perhaps for this reason that Soep and Chávez claim that the production process, complex as it is with detailed sections of constructing interviews and journalistic writing, lays the foundations for learning rather than necessarily *is* the learning (108). Learning is expressed as series of qualities of personal efficacy (109–110), and a core part of the argument is to show how the setting can provide a different and unique fusion of opportunities to allow this learning to take place.

Summary

In this chapter we have contrasted two exemplary studies of youth learning in creative media contexts. In both situations, the self—the young people themselves—is a key resource for learning. In both cases, working on identity is a key aim, and in both cases a disciplined, progressive curriculum is offered as a route to this development process. *Cultural identity* may seem almost too simplistic a term, given the ways that ethnicity, class, local sociogeographies, and gender position the subjects in these studies, but nevertheless, how these projects leverage the cultural in young people's lives to create opportunities for learning makes them interesting and important. Despite being nearly 30 years apart, it is remarkable how these programs' institutional settings, both with production-based curricula, actually offer affordances that make this unusual kind of learning possible. They also point to ways how new subjects and ways of learning are tried out and then developed in not-school before being mainstreamed.

5 Language and Technology: Learning to Learn and Metalearning

In chapter 3 we encountered the idea of learning-to-learn. Sinha's study explored some of social dispositions and orientations by young learners toward learning as a way of exploring how learners position themselves in relation to their educational trajectories (Sinha 1999). Similarly, in some of the more anthropological accounts of how people define for themselves their progress as learners in schools (or workplaces, or even within other community settings), research has focused on how people orient themselves within social situations (Levinson, Foley, and Holland 1996). In both of these cases, learning-to-learn is offered as a form of what some would call "social capital" (Camras 2004; Field 2008): a set of values, habits, dispositions, or implicit understandings that underpin learning. A key impulse behind much of the after-school and community programs has been the desire to provide precisely this sort of social capital to those denied it through economic inequality. And, indeed, there is a tradition of not-school programs aiming to supplement learning-to-learn capabilities.

In the most general sense, *metalearning* encompasses the idea of *learning-to-learn*, and both terms have both general, common-sensical as well as more restricted and specialist definitions. In this chapter, I will review studies that have explored how not-school works to support these more general learning capacities or capabilities.

We will focus on studies of language use, language being the touchstone (and, some might say, the be-all and end-all) of learning-to-learn. Studies explore how not-school experiences have helped pupils to develop linguistic abilities, sometimes conceptualized as language skills. The other extensive domain of activity relates to the uses of technologies in after-school and community settings. As discussed in the preceding chapter, media production is clearly technology dependent, but the case studies in this chapter are more explicitly computer-focused and rest on a premise that computer technologies offer a unique opportunity for pupils to construct knowledge and develop modes of thought. There is a long tradition of scholarship investigating how computers have been imagined in educational terms as mind-machines, in that they offer a direct vehicle for developing thinking (Greenfield 1984).

The Fifth Dimension and the Computer Clubhouse

The two most established technology-based after-school initiatives, the Fifth Dimension and Computer Clubhouse, have been around for 20 to 30 years. As both initiatives have developed over that time, they have also changed, especially with respect to working with the realities of underserved children in inner-city urban environments. They are both keen to stress that what may have begun with specific objectives has changed to accommodate the individual trajectories of their clientele. Nevertheless, both initiatives are led by universities working with community, and both were motivated by a strong theory of learning. The Fifth Dimension is rooted in neo-Vygotskian theory and explicitly tries to support learners move through a series of learning progressions, often using literacy, mathematical, and scientific curricula. Computer Clubhouse is rooted in Papertian constructivism, and offers structured play-like activities, often with customized computer technologies. Both programs have been around long enough to experience the trials of scaling as their programs have developed and become mainstreamed at a growing number of sites. Both programs additionally have expanded to offer other not-work-activity play and social functions to these original aims (Vásquez 2003). Equally, both programs have extended their area of interest to include benefits and outcomes for a range of university-based scholars and students. As digital technology itself has developed over this period, both initiatives have sought to extend their infrastructure and curricula, making the technology as current and as culturally sophisticated as possible.

I want, however, to set some of these broader considerations of program impact and function aside and concentrate on how technology use and curricula have been explored in relation to framing the development of metalearning.

Fifth Dimension does include large-scale, long-term quantitative analysis of effects. A 2006 study claims that participation improves cognitive and academic skills, further suggesting

"Fifth Dimension activity helps children develop skills in many domains . . . including computer usage, mathematical understanding, language and reading" (Cole and the Distributed Literacy Consortium 2006, 105). On the one hand, we have a focus on core capabilities (computer use, reading, and so on) that facilitate academic success and at the same time an interest in allying as closely as possible Fifth Dimension activity with conventional schooling. The authors go on to say: "when engaged in tasks whose format and content were modeled on Fifth Dimension activities . . . children improved in their performances." In other words, where school itself was like Fifth Dimension, performance measurably improved. One key argument is that "children can learn when they are invested in the goals of a task and motivated to participate in challenging activities" (106). From this point of view Fifth Dimension clearly offers its success as an argument for curriculum reform—that it isn't a question of out-of-school learning but ways of showing how school itself might be reformed in Fifth Dimensions' image.

In more detailed analysis of the "dynamics of change in children's learning." Fifth Dimension does offer classic formulations of how play and learning can be mediated, how "heterogeneous players—that is, adults and computer persona—and other children all acting in different authority/learner roles" and the uses of carefully structured, customized software all contribute toward quality of progression and attention in these after-school sessions. At the same time, the not-school social relations—that is, more personally interested kinds of "experienced" and "beginner" actors—also set up a kind of social learning that goes to the heart of supporting capabilities and learning-to-learn outcomes (chapter 6).

In the context of this report, it could be argued that Fifth Dimension is a very school-like not-school, and indeed that is a key part of its ambitions. Working with younger children in after-school rather than youth in community provision, as in the previous chapter, also underlines how difficult it is to talk about the institutional form of the sector, as clearly the regimen of after-school in this instance has very clear aspirations. This is even more apparent in the discussion of mainstreaming and scaling up Fifth Dimension (Cole and Distributed Literacy Consortium 2006, chapter 8) where reconfiguring definitions of learning to fit funders' priorities at times clashed and other times supported the model of learning promoted by organizing activities in the Fifth Dimension way.

The Computer Clubhouse also found that as it developed and spread, it too took on a wider social and civic function than it might have initially anticipated; entering the business of managing provision for children inevitably complicates things. As noted above, the key to Clubhouse is a constructivist model of learning, which is explicitly contrasted with instruction (Kafai, Peppler, and Chapman 2009, 19). Activities revolve around making and developing with digital technologies, and participation is organized around a "creative design spiral" (21) of creating → making → reflecting, which leads to further making. Most activities are in some ways digitally mediated, although robotics and other kinds of circuit-instruction-based technologies in addition to specialized software, especially the well-known "Scratch,"[12] are part of the offer. Although it is difficult to generalize, I have the impression that activities are less structured and perhaps offer more user choice than Fifth Dimension. The activities are, as we shall see, less centralized and while there is a curriculum, it seems less evident than in Fifth Dimension.

An interesting point of continuity between the work described in the previous chapter and Clubhouse are the questions of student choice, interest, and cultural buy-in. While Clubhouse is earnest about supporting members to build on their own interests, it doesn't always use a cultural model of identity as the starting point. This is not to say that finding ways to build on children's home and interests is ignored, and indeed there are some detailed studies of video game design and music videos that show how forms of popular-cultural consumption are built on in Clubhouse activities (Kafai and Peppler 2011; Peppler and Kafai 2006; 2007). However, the notions of cultural interest espoused in Clubhouse aren't quite the same things as those explored in the media productions in youth settings. This may partly again be a question of age, but it also relates to the place of cultural expression in a constructivist paradigm. Interest here is much more a question of a starting point and a way of defining goal orientation than the sorts of identity dispositions we saw in the previous chapter. My point here is not in any way to disparage or rank Clubhouse versus Youth Radio, but I hope that the contrast helps us identify what we mean by terms such as *interest,* where we are as much finding ways to describe qualities of participation, the disposition of the learner within a pedagogic relationship, as we are talking about the quality of the learning.

Like Fifth Dimension, Clubhouse also offers itself as in some ways a mirror to conventional schooling. There is a strong sense of a supplementary curriculum, especially in relation to computer science and engineering (Kafai, Peppler, and Chapman

2009, 57), and in relation to issues around diversifying the IT workforce (69). Like Fifth Dimension, the ethos of Clubhouse experiences is collaborative and social, with a sense that it is through this mode of participation that high-quality learning occurs (77). Indeed, in some senses, learning is defined as participation, and participation thus becomes a form of learning. This might seem a loose formulation on one level, but it goes to the heart of learning-to-learn, in that adopting the role and identity of learners within these kinds of participatory frameworks encourages the development of a learning identity (Wortham 2005).

Clubhouse clearly tries to take on the challenge of identifying the learning for learners, and while Fifth Dimension offers a way of reflecting on progress as structured through the various kinds of interaction within the program, Clubhouse attempts to develop its own form of reflection, called Pearls. Pearls is a social-knowledge software that aims to encapsulate learners' reflections with its own cycle of design, evaluation, and redesign. Pearls aims to "prompt learners' reflective thinking by focusing attention on various epistemological aspects of their Clubhouse projects" (Kafai, Peppler, and Chapman 2009, 82). Discussion of this software points to how, what the authors call, "reflective fluency" characterizes lifelong learning (89), and how using Pearls as a pedagogic device demonstrates how interacting with technology can scaffold "deeper learning" (89). It goes to the heart of how engaging with Clubhouse can support metalearning. I would also like to note that slightly less formal feedback as part of the process is also highlighted in other studies (Peppler and Kafai 2006; 2007) as performing the same function.

The study of Pearls does raise a key dilemma that underscores the discussion in this chapter so far—namely, whether forms of metalearning or learning-to-learn can be imagined distinctly from forms of formal learning. "Pearl design requires time and effort" (Peppler and Kafai 2007, 88). At times the authors suggest it took as long to produce these reflections as the work on which the reflecting was based. This is based on a very different economy of effect found in the not-school sector with its more casual, voluntary, and peripatetic experiences. The advocates of these programs are caught in a double bind. Learning, they would argue, is really about the process of reflection, how experience can be transformed. However, this is precisely what school does within a graded system of evaluation and controlled progression. The projects in the previous chapter found a way to integrate reflection within the process by which making meaning is shared with others—a process some Clubhouse scholars in particular observe through case studies (Peppler and Kafai 2007).

Language in and through the Arts

In a series of studies on the late 1990s and the early years of this century, Shirley Brice Heath explored how participating in youth arts, primarily drama and visual arts, creates a productive context for learning. Brice Heath and her colleagues paid considerable attention to the wider instrumental effects of participating in the arts, mainly in not-school settings, in order to tease out the wider benefits of such learning and especially to understand some of the metalearning processes we have tracked in this chapter. While technology provides the domain in Clubhouse and to an extent drives Fifth Dimension, Brice Heath and her colleagues focused on linguistic competence and how the particular experiences of participating in arts learning could be analyzed as a wider linguistic performance—which in turn could be argued to underpin a whole host of broader learning outcomes.

Heath, Soep, and Roach (1998) make a series of quantitative claims about how participating in such programs increased attendance and performance in general types of school-based participation and activity. The argument here is that participation itself increases other kinds of joining in and putting oneself forward. If not quite learning-to-learn qualities, these are akin to a set of similar preconditions. The authors then suggest that three particular kinds of verbal activities are more common in young people who participate in these settings. These verbal activities support a set of creative and critical faculties and include "theory-building and checking the possible," "translating and transforming," and "projecting and reflecting" (5). These are rooted in arts practices, and the authors suggest "become habituated for young artists" (8). They perform a meta-learning function. They argue that such linguistic use can be traced to the ways that community youth organizations are structured, how activities are organized, and how an ethos is developed. The authors go on to suggest that the languages of planning, critique, and evaluation derived directly from the arts activities are fostered by participating in them (14).

These arguments have been further elaborated and developed in succeeding work (Heath 2000; 2001; Heath and Roach 1999). In her contribution to the influential *Champions of Change* (Heath and Roach 1999), Brice Heath suggests a specific set of language use that she traces back to community arts work. These include "a fivefold increase of 'if-then statements,' scenario building following 'what if' questions; more than a twofold increase in use of mental state verbs (consider, understand, etc.); a doubling in the number of modal verbs (could, might, etc.)" (27). This observation is then developed into a series of learning strategies (what we might think of as metalearning approaches here), which, in addition to those mentioned earlier, can be added "creating analogies, demonstrating, negotiating, and exemplifying" (28). In a further study Brice Heath explored the effect of the taking on roles for performance at work (Heath 2000).

Summary

Brice Heath's work has been especially influential in the policy arena. Being able to claim this kind of learning, moving from valuing the intrinsic qualities of participation and circumventing the frequently contested status of the arts, to a metric where metalearning can be measured in terms of changing language use has been important in influencing skeptics. Like the studies of Fifth Dimension and Computer Clubhouse, Brice Heath represents a long-standing sociocultural tradition working in schools and formal education. However, by applying these learning outcomes to the not-school sector and in all three cases being able to find a generic capability (Alexander 2008) that derives directly from the particularities of the learning in these settings, proponents of the sector now have a different kind of legitimacy in educational circles.

6 In-Formal Learning: Traversing Boundaries

Readers may have noticed that so far I have elided non-formal and in-formal learning. I have done so mainly because I am concentrating on learning in and around forms of institutions that are, broadly speaking, educational, if not actually schools. So far, we have examined only general kinds of informal learning associated with culture, style, and other kinds of identity work. In this chapter I want to concentrate on more traditionally disciplined forms of in-formal learning—that is, learning pursued in the home and in leisure activities—and see how those experiences and kinds of learning are developed in not-school surroundings. My focus is on organized social practices that are, in crucial ways, extended and developed in not-school institutions.

There isn't a great deal of research exploring these issues, as designing and developing such enquiries is difficult and expensive, which is unfortunate because a key interest in contemporary digital cultures and the possibilities they appear to open up for young people are situated precisely at this boundary as much as they are interested in how out-of and in-school experiences might intersect.

The focus in this chapter is thus slightly more speculative then the previous two, but I aim here to begin to model some of the issues where at home and leisure forms of learning practices intersect with the semiformal but organized world of not-schools.

Amateur Musicians, Young Filmmakers, and Symbolic Creativity

Playing music is an especially interesting domain to explore in the context of this study for a number of reasons. As is well known, music and musical taste is a particularly intense and significant area of meaning and identity work for the young (and indeed the rest of us) (Thornton 1995; DeNora 2000). As has been noted by a number of commentators, playing music is a stratified activity on an amateur to professional continuum; furthermore, many musicians (or people who make music) learn to play or compose in relatively informal ways and are self-taught or learn in non-formal communities of practice (Finnegan 2007; Green 2002; 2008). Some musical genres are rooted in these community based amateur traditions. However, the formal discipline of music making and in particular the role of musical notation, along with the ideas of musical literacy, are equally powerful influences on the production of music making.

Scholars of music education have pointed out these contradictions, especially projects led by Lucy Green in the United Kingdom (Green 2008), and have been involved in the development of curricula that are explicitly rooted in these out-of-school and informal traditions of music making.[13] In this work, the relationship between in- and out-of school is reversed, as it were, with the curriculum and pedagogy in school being modeled on informal practices: learning through repetition, playing a part accompanied by a tape, choosing favorite songs, and so forth. The mechanisms by which these long-standing traditions have worked are then developed within the school curriculum and overlaid with formal knowledge—as opposed to the other way round.

The roles played by not-school in these processes is also interesting. The Scandinavian study *In Garageland* (Fornas, Lindberg, and Sernhede 1995) followed the development and growth of young bands (aged 14 and older) within youth clubs and at home, where youth-led settings determined participation and what we might describe as work habits—that is, how the groups come together, practice, rehearse, compose, and take their first performance steps—were molded in not-school surroundings.

Several of the case study bands in *In Garageland* worked out of youth centers. In Scandinavia in general, youth provision often involves young people at a governance level to a high degree and places greater emphasis on handing over resources, activities, and management to youth themselves. Their modus operandi stem from philosophies of peer learning, where being with other young people in purposive activity without extensive adult presences or direction is seen as a productive route to greater social and civic understanding:

The educational system especially is caught in this challenge of individualization in late modern society. It should secure both the broad societal interests in the development of social responsibility and support the individual subjectivity as the prerequisite of activity. The solutions to this challenge go in many directions. One solution is that children and young persons must solve the problems themselves. They have to develop their own trajectories. (Mørch 2006, 10)

This is a very different practice from the structured and organized activities we observed in the previous chapter, and we shall return to these theories of youth-driven work in the conclusion.

Deriving from a mixture of these approaches to youth learning and the embodied practices of music making itself, *In Garageland* develops a wider theory of learning in making rock music (the observed bands) along three dimensions. These are "learning in the external world," which, the authors point out, is traditionally the domain of school (Fornas, Lindberg, and Sernhede 1995, 232) encompassing practical competence, administrative abilities, and knowledge of nature and society; "learning in the shared world," the inter-subjective shared processes involving cultural skills, emotive capabilities, and relationship skills; and finally, "learning in the inner world," involving self-knowledge, the ability to form ideals directed toward goals, and expressive abilities (229–242). These features contain a high degree of the practical, the social, and the intrapersonal and clearly belong to a language or a philosophy of the self in society that may be slightly different from the Anglo-American tradition.

Not only does this study support the ways in which the disciplines and wider social practices surrounding organized out-of-school practices develop original ways of learning, but it also supports the unique contribution not-school settings can add to this mix. The authors are interested in the wider social practices of music making, but in their characterization of the social spaces available to the young, they do create a rich picture of learning spaces as a kind of ecology where family, schools, social life, community, and youth clubs all provide distinctive contributions to the possibilities for learning.

The idea of amateurism—although it is an ugly and problematic term—is part of this mix. Proponents of the network society and the empowering possibilities in digital technologies have tended to emphasize the shifting boundaries between definitions of professionals and amateurs—that they have become increasingly blurred as those with techie hobbies and interests become more specialized and passionate about their work (Leadbeater and Miller 2004). In some cases, not-school contexts (as in the case of the ARK, the youth center in *In Garageland*), are intermediate testing grounds for this amateur/professional continuum. This is certainly the case for Youth Radio, discussed in chapter 4,where I raised the idea of not-school as an R&D testing ground for curricula. Sometimes it is the mix of the social and the access to resources that comes to the fore, but at other organizations, it is how they bring together shared interests—a theme prominent in the *In Garageland* study. In a parallel fashion, Øystein Gilje has offered an analysis of young filmmakers who contributed to a Scandinavian site precisely for young filmmakers, dvoted.net.

Established (but now closed down) as an opportunity to bring together and promote filmmaking among young people, dvoted.net as an online site becomes the locus for not-school (Gilje 2013). According to Gilje, it provided a focus for ambition and a way of leveraging hobby-ism to more full-fledged amateur status. It is, however, Gilje's study of how young filmmakers (aged 16 to 19) move into serious creative identities that interest us here, and especially the interaction between self-motivated activity and more organized public works.

In Gilje's study, young filmmakers, who have the opportunity to complete this subject at school within a formal curriculum as well as contribute to and participate in the dvoted.net community, reflect on their formation as filmmakers. He found that some young people need to position themselves against the identity offered by the school subject, Media and Communication, and also that the kinds of knowledge prioritized in the school militated against other definitions of practice circulating in the filmmaking community. However, an appeal to an authentic arts self forged in the experience of auto-didacticism and developed though peer support was important. The students were interested in comparing experiences of equipment and technique as well as how making films for amateur or semi-professional purposes (such as local community events) were valued against school knowledge. Gilje is agnostic about this comparison, and it remains unclear how these attitudes support or hinder these young people as they move from school into further education and whether such identities are necessary or will change over time. From our point of view, it is interesting on two counts. First is how the creative identity formed through experience and participation might need to be counterpoised to the more conventional good-student identity. Second is how practical community knowledge has its own currency. Rather than the model pursued by Green (2008), where informal knowledge might be curricularized and then revisited out of school, suggesting an ongoing process of validation, here in the work of these young filmmakers, the kinds of knowledge privileged by these actors do not seem to find validation within formal knowledge domains. It is precisely the ability of not-school—in Gilje's case, a virtual one—to validate these kinds of informal knowledge as a practical commonsense aesthetic that makes the not-school locations so important within the economies of knowledge for these communities.

Both of these kinds of analysis return us to the work of Paul Willis mentioned in chapter 2 (Willis 1990). Willis's notion of "symbolic creativity" hypothesizes forms of knowledge that have their practices and values rooted in a range of social domains. Rather than thinking of learning as always being trapped in a process of incorporation from the in-formal or non-formal *to* the formal, Willis suggests that different kinds of knowledge derive their validity from within different social contexts. Although his work was at the level of peer or community organization and touched only on youth clubs in a peripheral fashion, barely mentioning a loose not-school formulation, as well as predating the Internet, we can see from our studies of learning music and filmmaking how productive a *diversity of provision* might be in sustaining a range of learning processes.

Tracing Biographies: Life Histories and Pathways

Gilje takes a loose biographical approach, interviewing subjects about pathways taken and choices made as people negotiate the educational system. This kind of approach is much more common in studies of adult learners and lifelong learning, where a sense of history and the subjects' ability to reflect on life-course trajectories may be seen as having validity and good local understanding.[14] There is a strong intellectual tradition analyzing how people make sense of their lives though these processes of identity making, or "biographicity" (Alheit 2009; West et al. 2007). Although the studies in chapter 5 examined learning specifically from the perspective of education scholars, and in chapter 4 how those scholars theorized learning albeit by drawing on insights and perspectives offered by participants, the life-history and biographical approach is more inclined to see how institutions work during the life course and how the meaning of learning unfolds over time, especially in relation to key issues at different life stages (Goodson and Sikes 2001). The ability to offer longer-term perspectives on the meaning of different experiences in different institutional or personal settings is a major contribution of this approach.

I haven't found studies exclusively devoted to people's experiences of learning outside school as a primary focus of scholarship (excepting Ashley 2009), but it is possible to aggregate insights as they appear in other studies. Again, it is difficult to explore cross-domain experiences. I would suggest three categories of study here: interviews with important actors in not-school worlds that focus on their reflections about their educational pathways, especially leaders and community activities; those literacy studies that are rooted in participants' life worlds; and studies of youth that focus on cross-domain experiences.

In chapter 3 we examined some of the work of Millbury McLaughlin, looking at her important studies of youth community provision. In her work and also in that of Hirsch (Hirsch 2005), we noted the key role played by adults in the interpersonal learning landscape offered in not-school environments (Heath and M. W. McLaughlin 1993; M. McLaughlin, Irby, and Langman 1994; M. W. McLaughlin 1999). The qualities of the adults working in these environments is seen as crucial to the success of these projects and as a key part of many of these adults' formation; their identities and capabilities stem from their own educational experiences, often in the community-based, not-school sectors. In studies of what makes these adults so influential, McLaughlin and colleagues often note that it is these adults' unconventional routes in life that make them such successful pedagogues. And although scholarship might seem more interested in these characters for what they offer to youth, we can see how it is their experience as learners and the biographical history of their learning that makes them so distinctive. In chapters 3 and 4 of *Urban Sanctuaries* (M. McLaughlin, Irby, and Langman 1994), for example, the authors offer portraits of contemporary community leaders. In nearly all cases, these adults found their own paths through experiences in not-school organizations and, in particular, used these experiences as stepping stones to further formal education and/or some kind of rescue from the streets. It is, however, the paradoxes contained in the idea of in-formal discipline, the home-grown institutions that offered these leaders important experiences in their youth and that they have come to embody as they act as leaders for the new younger generation. Even leaders who come from outside the communities in which they are now working seem to have been forged in not-school environments, and thus give us some insight into the role that such places can play in the overall life history of individuals (chapters 4 and 6).

One such community centered organization is the Digital Storytelling center (DUSTY) in Oakland, founded and researched by Glynda Hull and others over the past 10 to 15 years (see, for example, Hull and Katz 2006; Nelson and Hull 2008). Work in this tradition belongs within wider sociocultural analysis of literacy. Hull and her colleagues have been particularly interested in in how access to not-school settings has offered opportunities for creative self-expression through the provision of audience, technologies, and focus. Work has been especially focused on how the kinds of writing enabled by a more open curriculum in this kind of not-school setting can enable the "voicing [of] agentive selves through the creation of multimodal texts"(Hull and Katz 2006, 71). On another level, it engages with a wider debate about what constitutes effective and purposeful literacy education. At the same time, the authors of this study are not only keen to make case that the special nature of out-of-school provision can facilitate these more extended and powerful examples of writing but also that working at these kinds of centers enables a quality of engagement with life story and with a sense of self traversing a number of educational sites. One of the key research subjects, Randy, appears in a series of studies and repeatedly refers to how important DUSTY is to his sense of self, how participating in activities and making media are deeply fulfilling, and that the researchers could not possibly understand how meaningful these experiences have been to him (Hull and Katz 2006, 53). The researchers don't necessarily take these claims at face value, but by being able to contextualize the not-school experiences within both an overall life and the other educational pathways within it, they make a persuasive case that learning in these settings plays an important and possibly unique role. The ways that these kinds of life experiences can be mediated by the cultural forms on offer are much in the youth, photography tradition we examined in chapter 4, but in this analysis they derive different impetus from being contextualized in a biographical (and autobiographical) perspective.

There are a few (although not recent) quantitative studies of what I referred to as *domain crossing studies*. In *Arts in Their View* (Harland, Kinder, and Hartley 1995), the authors examine participation in the arts both in and out of school and get a view of how practices empower youth across all kinds of learning experiences. This isn't necessarily a form of biographical identity making, but it does capture how diverse experiences of learning in different institutional settings support, complement, hinder, or block each other. In chapter 12 the authors experiment with what they called *arts biographies,* matching categories of leisure with school or work and plotting experiences at different levels of schools, youth clubs, and current and future interests. This led to a typology of what the authors called an "attitude quota," where they plotted individuals' (mainly aged 16 and older) positive and negative attitudes in terms of task orientation, self-identity, therapeutic aims, ability, and status orientations. They built up a series of cameos to work out what were the greatest influences and barriers to participation (this was the policy context for the study). From our perspective, the study is of interest because of the way it plots practice and interests from the individual's point of view and how these might then be enabled or not across different social and institutional settings—including not-school experiences. The individual becomes the locus for the research perspective. Current research interest in young people's literacy practices across on- and offline worlds, between school and at home (see, for example, Leander and McKim [2003]; Leander, Phillips, and Headrick Taylor [2010]) also places the kinds of learning going on across different institutional settings in a person-centered perspective. This attempt to frame different kinds of learning from the learner's perspective underpins several ongoing research projects investigating these questions.[15]

Summary

This chapter explores approaches to developing learning across different social and institutional settings, in particular looking at how in-formal learning developed in the home, by one's self or as part of an interest-driven community might be valorized and further developed through not-school experiences. These ideas contrast to the thrust of much educational research that explores how such interests might be turned into curriculum by formal schooling. Although there isn't much research on these issues, I have suggested that an attention to biography and to the construction of the learning self might be a productive way forward in exploring these issues. Underpinning these analysis has been the insight that a socially productive learning culture requires the offer of a diverse ecology of provision; not-schools as well as formal education systems need to offer a way of validating learning rather than simply incorporating it—as in what appears to be the contemporary tendency to curricularize all kinds of out-of-school activities.

7 Conclusion

The English sociologist of education Basil Bernstein once famously noted that "schools cannot compensate for Society" (Bernstein 1970). As I have worked my way through the argument of this essay, I am tempted to remark ruefully that not-schools cannot compensate for schools either. In other words, some of the burden of aspiration that we all heap on formal education cannot and should not be placed on the non-formal sector either. We need to be cautious about how investing in and developing the non-formal learning sector can and cannot compensate or even remediate some the challenges evident in public education systems. In particular, I have paid attention to the distinctive features in the kinds of learning found in the non-formal sector, or what I have called *not-school*, to help us understand the sector better and imagine how it might contribute to the broader ecology of learning opportunities available to young people today.

The main aim of this report has been to review key directions in the literature and address what it might mean to talk about learning in the non-formal sector. I have raised the question of

how the institutions within this sector, which can be defined by
what they are not—school—might offer an institutional frame
for characterizing a type of learning. Most of the literature is
cautious about this idea, and reverting to broad sociocultural
theories, offers notions like participation structures to explain
the quality of learning enabled by organized out-of-school
learning. Although it has proven difficult to disentangle forms
of learning we know and take for granted from our school systems and from shared understanding of what it means to learn
and be educated, there are certain kinds of practices and ways of
engaging the inter- and intrapersonal self in learning activities
that do seem distinctive to the participation structures on offer.

We can summarize this attention to the self in terms of (a) a
mode of engaging, and valuing individual's sense of themselves
and (b) the quality of relationships between adult and peer. The
peer education philosophy, particularly prominent in northern
Europe, describes a "method for young people themselves to
develop a further understanding of modern youth life and their
own place and perspectives inside this."[16] Scholars like Rhodes
and Hirsch focus more on the semiformal mentoring roles available in organized settings (Hirsch 2005; Rhodes 2004). As we
have seen, a common focus is attention to the subjective well-
being of young people, their self-esteem, identity work, confi-
dence, interest in social outcomes, quality of relationships, and
other civic virtues—as well as of personal development well captured by the German concept of *bildung* (Chisholm 2008).

A number of theorists have commented on how the not-
school sector offers a distinctive kind of position within a
broader ecology of provision. McLaughlin and Hirsch refer to

this as a form of "intermediariness" of developing forms of social organization that deliberately and specifically sit between more traditional or conventional systems and structure (Hirsch 2005; M. W. McLaughlin et al. 2009).[17] We have also noted how the in-betweenness of the institutions also serve pathfinder functions, developing activity or curriculum that later might become incorporated into the mainstream. However, the tendency toward institutionalization—which many scholars suggest we need to be wary of as destroying the distinctiveness of the provision—is not always straightforward, and there is an absence of studies exploring the cost-benefit and indeed the plausibility of scaling up or mainstreaming from community-based innovation.

Historical and International Perspectives

A secondary ambition here has been to offer both a historical perspective on writing about not-school projects as well as to compare some international studies. One contention is that the sector is sufficiently developed—despite its precariousness in terms of sustainability, funding, and longevity—to allow for the value of alternative heuristics and especially those beyond local program evaluations.

One key background theme in our discussion has been the reframing of the meaning of lifelong (over time) and life-wide (across locations) learning. In a European context especially, scholarly discussion about lifelong learning has argued that individuals are now addressed with increasing urgency by policy having to both take responsibility for their own learning and to invest in themselves as economic resources to exploit changing employment opportunities (Edwards 1997; Griffin 2000). The terms of this discussion do impinge on some of the aspirations of the non-formal learning sector, as the politics of lifelong learning suggest a desire to maximize return on investment and that all forms of education—loosely, strongly, or narrowly defined—will become incorporated in this project of developing human capital.

Such a vision is quite contrary to the person-centeredness of much of the literature we have examined in previous chapters. It does, however, mesh with some of the historical trends identified toward the end of chapter 3.

There we described three key shifts in the literature about not-schools over the last twenty-five years. We noted a different kind of emphasis on the individual as opposed to the community as an object of intervention. This is not to say that current scholarship isn't interested in community but that the older literature more explicitly demonstrates its interest in groups, neighborhood, and community, whereas contemporary scholarship tends to focus at an individual level. Second, as observed in Hirsch's work, we can see the emergence of a debate around the instrumentalization of learning, as we have just described above, with a tendency to bring out economistic rather than social values—that is, being more interested in producing workers than citizens (Hirsch 2005). Writers like Hirsch are concerned that the kinds of spaces that are opened up in not-schools don't become overwhelmed by this changing agenda.

Finally, we have noted a tendency among policymakers and scholars alike to pedagogicize more and more of everyday life.

This is an ugly term that nonetheless captures the process whereby all interactions and transactions between children and adults are turned into opportunities for learning and developing educational outcomes. From this perspective, the very idea of in-formal learning may at times seem to threaten the sorts of boundaries that society deems appropriate for children and young people (Corsaro 2005).

Identity, Metalearning, and Embedded Practices

The discussion in chapters 3 through 6 have revolved around a nexus of ideas and practices that, although not offering a specialized theory of learning has nevertheless answered the question posed in the introduction: what might be the generic features of learning within the frames associated with this field? I have offered a reading of scholars who have examined creative media-making production practices, exploring the place of identity in curriculum activity and, above all, a way of working with people as learners so that broad underlying capacities can be realized and developed. As noted earlier, this report attempts to characterize the value of developing the inter- and intrapersonal self, which has been so central to the mission and purpose of not-school activities.

However, it has proven more complex to answer the question: what are the traditions and conventions of pedagogy at work in organized out-of-school settings? Many of the studies cited have found it quite straightforward to address curricula in these contexts; and whether they have invoked youth-work traditions or, as we have seen, the studio or media practice, the out-of-school settings themselves haven't been a major issue. It may be that such concerns are not that salient for enquiry in this field.

Given, as I have argued, that much of the experiences of participation are valued precisely because of what they are not (school) and made meaningful through contrast and comparison within any individual's learning ecology, I suggest that a key function of analysis of this sector is that it enables us to see how modes of learning may or may not be transferred across experiences. It helps us raise deep challenges in understanding what it means to talk about the quality of learning pertaining to these experiences (Sefton-Green 2004). As observed in chapter 2, helping us think about learning as a set of plural activities rather than an individualized unitary mode may be a an important critical implication of study in this area. However, being able to reflect on when and where we are applying a common sense of what constitutes learning as derived from experiences of schooling always needs to be brought back into perspective.

In chapter 7 of *Between Movement and Establishment* (M. W. McLaughlin et al. 2009), the authors attempt to identify conceptually different ways of explaining change to understand at a theoretical level how to describe and analyze social innovations. They use the idea of "cultural frames" and "social logics" (chapter 7). We need a similar way of theorizing this new discourse about learning to enable us to get a grip on how not-schools might be able to legitimize the kinds of learning they espouse: in McLaughlin et al.'s terms, to examine whether any of these kinds of learning represent a type of "in-betweenness" (8). Part of the challenge in this report has been to describe a conceptually new landscape of learning that can be captured only by more established educational language. Although this might always be the destiny of any radical movement, the issue here is contemporary, and our understanding of what learning is and what might be possible is always going to be determined by the tone and flavor of educational discourse around us—and that varies from culture to culture, possibly from country to country.

Implication for Further Study

This conceptual dilemma isn't helped by empirical weaknesses and absences in the research literature. Chapter 3 contains a series of criticisms of the reach (especially in terms of international and intra-nation spread and depth) and composition of the research field. Even if there was some agreement about the mix of identity-based, person-centered, production-based curriculum and pedagogy, the unanswered questions about the institutional frame, participation structures, and indeed the place of not-schools within the wider ecology of education provision include:

• What defines progression, or, for that matter, achievement? Is there a place for accreditation?
• What does the learning mean to the teachers (if that's always the correct term) in this sector? Or to the learners? In what ways is it defined as learning or education, especially if as noted above, there is tension between the limited language of learning available and the desire to develop conceptually or strategically new or different kinds of educational experiences?

• Over what timescales—what life-trajectories—can we or do we make sense of the not-school experiences? How can we make connections between learning and outcomes such as employment? How can we connect learning in not-school situations to other kinds of educational experiences, especially if we are interested in learning-to-learn or metalearning capabilities?

• And especially, what are the points of correspondence with more conventional learning systems, definitions, vectors, and histories? How might the totality of learning experiences connect within and across people?

• Finally, if we are interested in community or neighborhood, how can we trace the experiences of participation and belonging at levels beyond the individual?

These are all difficult research questions. They also suggest that in some way focus needs shift away from the specifics of the sector (as much as possible at this time) and toward understanding the totality of learning across and within the lives of individuals and communities. That too is a tough challenge for research: but without evidence and informed theory, we run the risk of perpetuating naive advocacy and self-fulfilling evaluations.

Notes

1. http://data.worldbank.org/indicator/SE.XPD.TOTL.GD.ZS/
countries?display=graph.

2. The OECD's Centre for Research and Education has supported much work in this vein. See, for example, http://www.oecd.org/document/61/ 0,3746,en_2649_35845581_37425853_1_1_1_1,00.html; and publications such as Schuller et al. 2004, Schuller and Desjardins 2007.

3. See http://www.infed.org/biblio/b-socped.htm.

4. See the history recounted in http://www.infed.org/biblio/b-socped. htm; and resources at http://social-pedagogy.co.uk/index.htm.

5. I would speculate that this is likely because most studies of this sector are, as noted as the end of the last chapter, supplier-side-oriented—that is, paying attention to the deliverer, the organization, and quality of the provision rather than analyzing the experience from the learner's point of view.

6. For a history of the terms, see Colley, Hodkinson, and Malcolm. 2003 and Sefton-Green 2004.

7. See many of the examples collected in Mahiri (2003).

8. See http://www.eurodesk.org/edesk/EUToolbox.do?go=1 and http:// ec.europa.eu/youth/youth/doc152_en.htm.

9. See http://www.nya.org.uk.

10. We will see in chapter 5 how this model has been taken up in more detail, but it should be noted that there are also sociocultural approaches to this popular concept (e.g., Sinha 1999) exploring how learning might better be thought of at a metalevel rather than necessarily tied to any particular content.

11. See also Seiter 2005 for a wider contextual discussion including baby-sitting, cooking, and so on, in the context of out-of-school learning.

12. See http://scratch.mit.edu.

13. See especially http://www.musicalfutures.org.

14. http://www.tlrp.org/proj/phase111/biesta.htm.

15. http://www2.lse.ac.uk/media@lse/research/The%20Class.aspx or http://www.uv.uio.no/pfi/english/research/projects/erstad-learning -lives/index.html.

16. Sven Mørch, "Modern Peer Learning and Social Contexts," http://ec.europa.eu/youth/archive/doc/studies/youthforeurope/peer_education.pdf.

17. See also http://www.infed.org/archives/demos/inside_out.htm.

References

Alexander, J. M. 2008. *Capabilities and Social Justice: The Political Philosophy of Amartya Sen and Martha Nussbaum*. Aldershot, UK: Ashgate.

Alheit, P. 2009. "Biographical Learning: Within the New Lifelong Learning Discourse." In *Contemporary Theories of Learning: Learning Theorists in Their Own Words*, ed. K. Illeris. Abingdon, UK: Routledge.

Ashley, M. 2009. "Time to Confront Willis's Lads with a Ballet Class? A Case Study of Educational Orthodoxy and White Working-Class Boys." *British Journal of Sociology of Education* 30 (2): 179–191.

Bamford, A. 2006. *The Wow Factor: Global Research Compendium on the Impact of the Arts in Education*. Berlin: Waxmann Verlag GmbH.

Bekerman, Z., N. C. Burbules, D. S. Keller, and D. Silberman-Keller, eds. 2005. *Learning in Places: The Informal Education Reader*. New York: Peter Lang.

Bernstein, B. 1970. "Education Cannot Compensate for Society." *New Society* 15 (387): 344–347.

Boekaerts, M. 2010. "The Crucial Role of Motivation and Emotion in Classroom Learning." In *The Nature of Learning Using Research to Inspire Practice*, ed. H. Dumont, D. Istance, and F. Benavides. Paris: OECD.

Brown, J. S., and P. Duguid. 2000. *The Social Life of Information*. Boston: Harvard Business School Press.

Camras, M. 2004. "Investing in Social Capital Afterschool Activities and Social Affiliation in Immigrant Youth." *Afterschool Matters* 2: 20–41.

Chisholm, L. 2008. "Re-contextualising Learning in Second Modernity." In *Youth Transitions: Processes of Social Inclusion and Patterns of Vulnerability in a Globalised World*, ed. R. Bendit and M. Hahn-Bleibtreu. Leverkusen: Barbara Budrich.

Coffield, F. 2000. *The Necessity of Informal Learning*. London: Policy Press.

Cole, M., and The Distributed Literacy Consortium. 2006. *The Fifth Dimension: An After-School Program Built on Diversity*. New York: Russell Sage Foundation.

Colley, H., P. Hodkinson, and J. Malcolm. 2003. "Informality and Formality in Learning: A Report for the Learning and Skills Research Centre." Learning Skills Research Centre, University of Leeds.

Corsaro, W. A. 2005. *The Sociology of Childhood*. Thousand Oaks, CA: Pine Forge Press.

DeNora, T. 2000. *Music in Everyday Life*. Cambridge: Cambridge University Press.

Dewdney, A., and M. Lister. 1988. *Youth, Culture, and Photography*. London: Palgrave Macmillan.

DICE Consortium. 2010. *The DICE Has Been Cast. Research Findings and Recommendations on Educational Theatre and Drama*. Brussels: European Commission.

Drotner, K., H. Jensen, and K. Schroder, eds. 2009. *Informal Learning and Digital Media*. Cambridge: Cambridge Scholars Press.

Edwards, R. 1997. *Changing Places? Flexibility, Lifelong Learning, and a Learning Society*. London: Routledge.

Edwards, R. 2009. "Introduction: Life as a Learning Context." In *Rethinking Contexts for Learning and Teaching: Communities, Activities, and Networks*, ed. R. Edwards, G. Biesta, and M. Thorpe. London: Routledge.

Edwards, R., G. Biesta, and M. Thorpe, eds. 2009. *Rethinking Contexts for Learning and Teaching: Communities, Activities, and Networks*. London: Routledge.

Eraut, M. 1994. *Developing Professional Knowledge and Competence*. London: Routledge.

Felstead, A., D. Bishop, A. Fuller, N. Jewson, L. Unwin, and K. Kakavelakis. 2007. "Performing Identities at Work: Evidence from Contrasting Sectors." Paper first presented to the "Transitions through the Lifecourse" seminar series, University of Nottingham, October 2006.

Field, J. 2008. *Social Capital*. London: Routledge.

Finnegan, R. 2007. *The Hidden Musicians: Music-Making in an English Town*. London: Wesleyan University Press.

Fornas, J., U. Lindberg, and O. Sernhede. 1995. *In Garageland: Rock, Youth, and Modernity*. London: Routledge.

Freidson, E. 2001. *Professionalism: The Third Logic: On the Practice of Knowledge*. Chicago: University of Chicago Press.

Geertz, C. 1985. *Local Knowledge: Further Essays in Interpretive Anthropology*. New York: Basic Books .

Gilje, O. 2013. "Trajectories and Timescales: The Stories of Four Young Scandinavian Filmmakers." In *Identity, Community, and Learning Lives in the Digital Age*, ed. O. Erstad and J. Sefton-Green. Cambridge: Cambridge University Press.

Goodson, I. F., and P. J. Sikes. 2001. *Life History Research in Educational Settings: Learning from Lives*. Milton Keynes, UK: Open University Press.

Green, L. 2002. *How Popular Musicians Learn: A Way Ahead for Music Education*. Aldershot, UK: Ashgate.

Green, L. 2008. *Music, Informal Learning and the School: A New Classroom Pedagogy*. Aldershot, UK: Ashgate.

Greenfield, P. M. 1984. *Mind and Media: The Effects of Television, Computers and Video Games*. Cambridge, MA: Harvard University Press.

Griffin, C. (2000, October 28). "Lifelong Learning: Policy, Strategy and Culture." Working paper of the Global Colloquium on Supporting Lifelong Learning, Milton Keynes, UK. http://www.open.ac.uk/lifelong-learning.

Halverson, E. 2010. "Film as Identity Exploration: A Multimodal Analysis of Youth-Produced Films." *Teachers College Record* 112 (9): 2352–2378.

Harland, J., K. Kinder, and K. Hartley. 1995. *Arts in Their View: Study of Youth Participation in the Arts*. Slough, UK: National Foundation for Educational Research.

Heath, S. B. 2000. "Making Learning Work." *Afterschool Matters* 1:33–45.

Heath, S. B. 2001. "Three's Not a Crowd: Plans, Roles, and Focus in the Arts." *Educational Researcher* 30 (7): 10–17.

Heath, S. B., and M. W. McLaughlin. 1993. *Identity and Inner-City Youth: Beyond Ethnicity and Gender*. New York: Teachers College Press.

Heath, S. B., and A. Roach. 1999. "Imaginative Actuality: Learning in the Arts during the Non-School Hours." In *Champions of Change: The Impact of the Arts on Learning*, ed. E. Fiske. Washington, DC: Arts Education Partnership.

Heath, S. B., E. Soep, and A. Roach. 1998. *Living the Arts through Language-Learning: A Report on Community-Based Youth Organizations*. Stanford, CA: Carnegie Foundation for the Advancement of Teaching.

Hill, S. 2007. *Afterschool Matters: Creative Programs That Connect Youth Development and Student Achievement*. Thousand Oaks, CA: Corwin Press.

Hirsch, B. J. 2005. *A Place to Call Home: After-School Programs for Urban Youth*. New York: Teachers College Press.

Hodge, R., and G. Kress. 2007. *Social Semiotics*. Cambridge: Polity Press.

Holland, D., W. Lachicotte Jr.,D. Skinner, and C. Cain. 1998. *Identity and Agency in Cultural Worlds*. Cambridge, MA: Harvard University Press.

Hull, G., and M.-L. Katz. 2006. "Crafting and Agentive Self: Case Studies of Digital Storytelling." *Research in the Teaching of English* 1 (43): 41–81.

Hunter, I. 1994. *Rethinking the School: Subjectivity, Bureaucracy, Criticism*. London: Allen & Unwin.

Jenkins, H. 2006. *Convergence Culture: Where Old and New Media Collide*. New York: NYU Press.

Kafai, Y., and K. Peppler. 2011 "Youth, Technology, and DIY: Developing Participatory Competencies in Creative Media Production." *Review of Research in Education* 35 (1): 89–119.

Kafai, Y. B., K. A. Peppler, and R. N. Chapman. 2009. *The Computer Clubhouse: Constructionism and Creativity in Youth Communities*. New York: Teachers College Press.

Knobel, M., C. Lankshear, and C. Bigum. 2007. *A New Literacies Sampler*. New York: Peter Lang.

Lareau, A. 2003. *Unequal Childhoods: Class, Race and Family Life*. Berkeley: University of California Press.

Latour, B. 2007. *Reassembling the Social: An Introduction to Actor-Network-Theory*. Oxford: Oxford University Press.

Lave, J., and E. Wenger. 1991. *Situated Learning: Legitimate Peripheral Participation*. Cambridge: Cambridge University Press.

Leadbeater, C., and P. Miller. 2004. *The Pro-Am Revolution: How Enthusiasts Are Changing Our Society and Economy*. London: Demos.

Leander, K., and K. McKim. 2003. "Tracing the Everyday "Sittings" of Adolescents on the Internet: A Strategic Adaptation of Ethnography across Online Spaces." *Education Communication and Information* 3 (2): 211–240.

Leander, K., N. Phillips, and K. Headrick Taylor. 2010. "The Changing Social Spaces of Learning: Mapping New Mobilities."*Review of Research in Education* 34: 329–394.

Lemke, J. 2000. "Across the Scales of Time: Artifacts, Activities, and Meanings in Ecosocial Systems." *Mind, Culture, and Activity* 7 (4): 273–290.

Lemke, J. 2008. "Identity, Development, and Desire: Critical Questions." In *Identity Trouble: Critical Discourse and Contested Identities*, ed. C. R. Caldas-Coulthard and R. Iedema. London: Palgrave.

Levinson, B., D. Foley, and D. Holland. 1996. *Cultural Production of the Educated Person: Critical Ethnographies of Schooling and Local Practice.* Albany: State University of New York Press.

Mahiri, J. 2003. *What They Don't Learn in School: Literacy in the Lives of Urban Youth.* New York: Peter Lang.

McLaughlin, M. W. 1999. *Community Counts: How Youth Organizations Matter for Youth Development.* Washington, DC: Public Education Network.

McLaughlin, M., M. Irby, and J. Langman. 1994. *Urban Sanctuaries: Neighborhood Organizations in the Lives and Futures of Inner-City Youth.* San Francisco: Jossey-Bass.

McLaughlin, M. W., W. R. Scott, S. N. Deschenes, K. C. Hopkins, and A. R. Newman. 2009. *Between Movement and Establishment: Organizations Advocating for Youth.* Stanford, CA: Stanford University Press.

McLaughlin, T. 1996. *Street Smarts and Critical Theory: Listening to the Vernacular.* Madison: University of Wisconsin Press.

Mørch, S. 2006. "Learning to Become Youth: An Action Theory Approach." *Outlines* 1: 3–18.

Nelson, M. E., and G. Hull. 2008. "Self-Presentation through Multimedia: A Bakhtinian Perspective on Digital Storytelling." In *Digital Storytell-*

ing, Mediatized Stories: Self-Representations in New Media, ed. K. Lundby. New York: Peter Lang.

Peppler, K., and Y. Kafai. 2006. "Creative Codings: Investigating Cultural, Personal, and Epistemological Connections in Media Arts Programming." In *ICLS '06 Proceedings of the 7th International Conference on Learning Sciences*. Bloomington, Indiana. New York: ACM.

Peppler, K., and Y. Kafai. 2007. "From SuperGoo to Scratch: Exploring Creative Digital Media Production in Informal Learning." *Learning, Media and Technology* 32 (2): 149–166.

Pugh, A. 2009. *Longing and Belonging: Parents, Children, and Consumer Culture*. Berkeley: University of California Press.

Rhodes, J. 2004. "The Critical Ingredient: Caring Youth-Staff Relationships in After-School Settings." *New Directions for Youth Development* 101: 145–162.

Schegloff, E. 1997. "Whose Text? Whose Context." *Discourse & Society* 8 (2): 165–187.

Schuller, T., and R. Desjardins. 2007. *Understanding the Social Outcomes of Learning*. Paris: OECD.

Schuller, T., C. Hammond, A. Bassett-Grundy, J. Preston, and J. Bynner. 2004. *The Benefits of Learning: The Impact of Education on Health, Family Life and Social Capital*. Cambridge: Routledge Falmer.

Sefton-Green, J. 2004. *Literature Review in Informal Learning with Technology Outside School*. Bristol, UK: Futurelab.

Sefton-Green, J. 2006. "New Spaces for Learning: Developing the Ecology of Out-of-School Education." Hawke Research Institute Working Paper, Hawke Research Institute for Sustainable Societies, University of South Australia.

Seiter, E. 2005. *The Internet Playground: Children's Access, Entertainment, and Mis-Education*. New York: Peter Lang.

Sinha, C. 1999. "Situated Selves: Learning to Be a Learner." In *Learning Sites: Social and Technological Resources for Learning*, ed. J. Bliss, R. Saljo, and P. Light, 32–48. Oxford: Pergamon Press.

Soep, E., and V. Chávez. 2010. *Drop That Knowledge: Youth Radio Stories*. Berkeley: University of California Press.

Thornton, S. 1995. *Club Cultures: Music, Media, and Subcultural Capital*. Cambridge: Polity Press.

Vadeboncoeur, J. 2006. "Engaging Young People: Learning in Informal Contexts." In *Rethinking Learning: What Counts as Learning and What Learning Counts*, ed. J. Green and A. Luke, 239–278. Washington, DC: AERA.

Varenne, H. 2007. "Difficult Collective Deliberations: Anthropological Notes toward a Theory of Education." *Teachers College Record* 109 (7): 1559–1588.

Vásquez, O. 2003. *La clase magica*. New York: Lawrence Erlbaum.

Wenger, E. 1999. *Communities of Practice: Learning, Meaning, and Identity*. Cambridge: Cambridge University Press.

Werquin, P. 2010. *Recognising Non-Formal and Informal Learning: Outcomes, Policies, and Practices*. Paris: OECD Publishing.

Wertsch, J. V. 1997. *Mind as Action*. Oxford: Oxford University Press.

West, L., P. Alheit, A. S. Andersen, and B. Merrill. 2007. *Using Biographical and Life History Approaches in the Study of Adult and Lifelong Learning*. New York: Peter Lang.

Willis, P. E. 1990. *Common Culture: Symbolic Work at Play in the Everyday Cultures of the Young*. Milton Keynes, UK: Open University Press.

Wortham, S. 2005. *Learning Identity: The Joint Emergence of Social Identification and Academic Learning*. Cambridge: Cambridge University Press.